MAX WEBER

KEY SOCIOLOGISTS

Editor: Peter Hamilton
The Open University

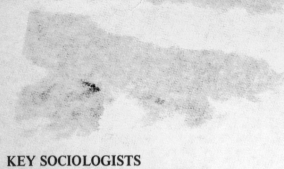

KEY SOCIOLOGISTS
Series Editor: PETER HAMILTON
The Open University, Milton Keynes

This series well present concise and readable texts covering the work, life and influence of many of the most important sociologists, and sociologically-relevant thinkers, from the birth of the discipline to the present day. Aimed primarily at the undergraduate, the books will also be useful to pre-university students and others who are interested in the main ideas of sociology's major thinkers.

MARX and Marxism
PETER WORSLEY
Professor of Sociology, University of Manchester

MAX WEBER
FRANK PARKIN
Tutor in Politics and Fellow of Magdalen College, Oxford

EMILE DURKHEIM
KENNETH THOMPSON
Reader in Sociology, Faculty of Social Sciences, The Open University, Milton Keynes

TALCOTT PARSONS
PETER HAMILTON
The Open University, Milton Keynes

SIGMUND FREUD
ROBERT BOCOCK
The Open University, Milton Keynes

THE FRANKFURT SCHOOL
TOM BOTTOMORE
Professor of Sociology, University of Sussex

C. WRIGHT MILLS
JOHN ELDRIDGE
Professor of Sociology, The University, Glasgow

MAX WEBER

FRANK PARKIN
Tutor in Politics and Fellow of
Magdalen College, Oxford

ROUTLEDGE
London and New York

First published in 1982 by Ellis Horwood Ltd
and Tavistock Publications Ltd

Reprinted 1982 and 1986

Reprinted 1988 by Routledge
11 New Fetter Lane, London EC4P 4EE
29 West 35th Street, New York, NY 10001

Typeset in Press Roman by Ellis Horwood Ltd
Printed in Great Britain by Richard Clay Ltd, Bungay, Suffolk

British Library Cataloguing in Publication Data

Parkin, Frank
  Max Weber.
  1. Weber, Max — Criticism and interpretation
  I. Title
  301'.092'4   HB107.W4
ISBN 0 415 03462 0

Table of Contents

Frank Parkin is a graduate of the London School
of Economics (B.A. Anthropology 1961; Ph.D.
Sociology 1966). From 1965 to 1975 he was
Lecturer, then Reader, in Sociology at the University
of Kent at Canterbury.

His publications include *Middle Class Radicalism*
(1968); *Class Inequality and Political Order* (1971);
The Social Analysis of Class Structure (Editor,
1975); *Marxism and Class Theory: A Bourgeois
Critique* (1979).

He is currently an Associate Editor of *Theory and
Society*, and a member of the editorial board of
the *American Journal of Sociology*.

Since 1975 Dr Parkin has been Tutor in Politics,
and Fellow of Magdalen College, Oxford.

Editor's Foreword

Max Weber, like his close contemporary Emile Durkheim (1858-1917) deserves a special place in any series devoted to *Key Sociologists*. Indeed his name is frequently combined with those of Durkheim and Karl Marx into a sort of secular trinity of sociologists deified wherever sociology is taught. Yet despite the apparent companionship of the trinity they appear on closer examination to be rather uneasy bedfellows. Marx was not strictly a sociologist – the label existed in his lifetime but could hardly be said to describe any recognisable discipline. This does not stop us from describing Marx as a Key Sociologist – indeed another book in this series is devoted to *Marx and Marxism* – primarily because what he wrote is central to the modern concerns of professional sociologists. Durkheim similarly does not share a great deal in common with Weber. Although both were academic sociologists the characteristic theories and methods of the two men set them at a considerable distance from each other. Even their approach to developing the new science of sociology differed fundamentally, Durkheim devoting his life to the patient work of creating the teaching institutions, learned societies and journals so essential to its institutionalization, whilst Weber was more of the pure scholar content to grapple with fundamental problems and from time to time come up with an inspirational idea that others could use. Typically, perhaps, he favoured the closed world of the private salon as the location of much of his teaching – when he could do it. For a lengthy period in the middle of his life mental problems robbed him of the ability to teach.

But Weber and Durkheim do share certain similarities. Both were concerned to develop a subject which would have appeared to Marx to be at best a highly partisan 'science' of society and at worst a 'bourgeois ideology'. When they began this work the discipline of sociology hardly possessed a solid European base at all (the situation was a little different in America). It had only a tenuous foothold in the otherwise very go-ahead German universities of the late 19th century – as witness the fact that Weber did not obtain a University post as a sociologist until relatively late in his life, coming to the subject from economics. Durkheim was faced with a similar situation in France and, like Weber, made the move into sociology from other academic areas – in his case philosophy and pedagogy.

Why then is Weber a *Key Sociologist*? The proper answer to that question is to be found in Frank Parkin's book, and I will not try to anticipate it here. A few general remarks are however worth making. Like Marx and Durkheim, Weber was responsible for the emergence of ideas which continue to be central to the development of the subject. Concepts like that of 'meaningful social action', 'ideal-type', forms of domination, and the stratification processes of societies, have been used and reworked by sociologists to approach a wide range of problems. Originally conceived at a time when the intellectual boundaries of sociology were very limited, these ideas have shown their power by retaining a currency through all the vicissitudes of the growing subject on its way to becoming an international science. Yet Weber's ideas are by no means simple complements to those of Marx and Durkheim; each wrote for a particular audience and with quite different aims in mind. This is why no matter what attempts are made to synthesise their theories they remain essentially contradictory – different *models* for apprehending the complexity of society. Weber's sociological models are different from those of his fellows in the trinity: they stress a methodological individualism opposed to both Marxian and Durkheimian constructs of social collectivities, a belief in the value of individual insight, and a lack of faith in the possibility of ever achieving irrevocable answers to sociological questions.

Whilst it is incontrovertible that Weber's work has influenced much of Western sociology, it has to be pointed out that it contains imprecisions and contradictions which have led to a range of different interpretations of his concepts and methods. Weber would not have been surprised at this, but it remains the case that the 'Weber' who is referred to as the source of this or that key formulation or typology is in effect a constantly changing character capable of being read in a number of different ways.

Thus the great merit of Frank Parkin's study is that it concentrates on the four central elements of Weber's *oeuvre* which have been most discussed and utilised by other sociologists. In turn he examines what Weber put forward as method or theory, and then provides a critique which illuminates both the strengths and contradictions of his sociology. And it is perhaps in his contradictions that Weber is most important for sociology. For in looking critically at what he said we can move on to develop sociological ideas which are an advance on Weber's. Sociology has pretensions, at the very least, to being a science – and no science can afford to treat the work of its key thinkers as inviolable and safe from criticism. It is only by exploiting the errors of its forebears that a science can progress. Frank Parkin's book shows very clearly why Weber holds a key position in the development of sociology, but at the same time why his ideas are stepping stones towards deeper insight about society.

Peter Hamilton

To John and Krishan

Preface

This essay takes another look at some of Weber's best known contributions to political and social theory. There is hardly anything in the main body of the text about Weber 'the man' – his career, his family life, his political doings, or his occasional bouts of madness. For those interested in these things I have provided a brief biographical sketch.

Four substantive areas of Weber's work are considered. Chapter One deals with his recommendations and pronouncements on method. Here a number of questions are raised about the procedural uses and application of *Verstehen* as a distinct mode of understanding, and about the explanatory claims made on behalf of ideal-type constructs. Weber's views on ethical neutrality and on historical explanation are also touched upon.

Chapter Two examines his treatment of the normative and institutional components of social action, with particular reference to religious beliefs and conduct. Some doubts are expressed about Weber's line of reasoning in seeking to establish a causal link between early Protestant beliefs and the rational capitalist mentality. There is also an attempt to demonstrate the tension between his analysis of Calvinism and the more 'materialist' stance that pervades his general sociology of religion.

Chapter Three considers his discussion of authority relations and the typology of domination. The suggestion is made here that Weber tends to muddy the distinction between legitimation and legitimacy, and that his sociology of domination is vitiated by the absence of a complementary sociology of compliance.

Chapter Four deals with his contribution to stratification theory. Some contrasts are drawn between Weberian and Marxist analyses of class and property relations, and conceptions of the state. Particular attention is given to Weber's ideas about status-group formations within the distributive set-up. The essay concludes with some comments on Weber's somewhat eccentric evaluation of the role of 'party' in the overall distribution of power.

Donald MacRae has said that "Practically all that is written on Weber is written in awe". I have tried not to let my own sense of awe at Weber's achievement degenerate into reverence. Most of the arguments set out in the following pages were first aired in a series of lectures and seminars given at various times in Oxford, Berkeley, and New York University. I am most grateful to the teachers and graduate students at these places for their often successful efforts to show me the error of my ways.

Magdalen College, Oxford
September, 1981   F.P.

Biographical Sketch

Max Weber was born in 1864 in Erfurt, once a Hanseatic town, now part of the German Democratic Republic. Soon after his birth the family moved to Berlin where their home became a talking shop for local academics, businessmen, artists and political big-wigs. The young Weber would have found it hard to avoid having to listen to a good deal of cultured and high-minded chatter, as well as no doubt to some less than enlightened political views. After taking his *Abitur* he enrolled as a student of jurisprudence at Heidelberg University. There he seems to have gone in for all the conventional Student Prince activities: a little studying, a lot of drinking and carousing, and trying (successfully) to have his face slit open in the duelling hall.

After a year out for military service he resumed his studies, first in Berlin, then in Göttingen. Here he knuckled down to serious work. In 1889 he completed his doctoral dissertation on medieval trading companies and two years later presented his *Habilitationsschrift* on some aspects of Roman agrarian history. This formally qualified him for a university appointment and he duly took up a post as law lecturer in Berlin. After a couple of years he moved on to Freiburg and then, in 1896, back to Heidelberg.

It was at Heidelberg that his troubles began. In 1898 he suffered a nervous breakdown that cut short his university career just as it was beginning to blossom. It was several years before he was able to resume any scholarly work, and the rest of his academic life was spent as a kind of prolonged sabbatical. His illness occurred soon after the death of his father. Weber senior was by all accounts a bad caricature of the Victorian paterfamilias — a martinet to his children, overbearing and insensitive towards his wife. Shortly before his death he and Max had quarrelled violently. It was something to do with the son's insistence that his mother be allowed to visit him unaccompanied by his father, whom he regarded as a bit of a lout. The row culminated in Weber junior doing the unthinkable thing of ordering his father from the house. Max never saw his father alive again. On learning of the old man's sudden death he was consumed by guilt and remorse. He then became virtually catatonic. Weber and Freud never met, but it is not hard to guess how Freud would have diagnosed Weber's malady.

Unable to concentrate on anything, Weber took refuge in travel. He was now forever packing his bags and hurrying to catch trains and steamers. His destinations were mainly in southern Europe, Italy in particular, but in 1904 he went further afield, making his one trip to the United States. He was enthralled by the pace and tumult of life in the big cities and by the strange democratic customs of the natives. There was much that he admired about America and he affected none of the haughty disdain for the vulgarity of the place, so common among visiting European intellectuals.

The New World, for its part, must have done him some good, for on his return home he started to work again. He quickly completed his essays on method and on the Protestant ethic. He taught himself Russian and within a matter of months had a sufficient grasp of contemporary sources to write a piece on the 1905 revolution. Once set in motion his vast productive energies knew no cease, despite mild recurrences of his melancholia. There followed a succession of studies dealing with legal institutions, religious systems, political economy, and authority relations that in their comparative scope and wealth of documentation have never been surpassed. Nor are they now ever likely to be. Given the quantum growth in each of the various disciplines that Weber felt at home in, no one person will ever be equipped to bestride the fields of law, history, and the social sciences with anything approaching his comprehensive mastery.

His scholarly output was brought to a temporary halt by the onset of war in 1914. He was fifty at the time and too old to take part in the fighting, much to his regret. Instead he was put in charge of hospital administration in his home town, not the most glamorous of tasks for a man who craved to be in the thick of the action. It is not easy to picture Weber as a Prussian version of Florence Nightingale, though he seems to have enjoyed playing the part. After a year or so he gave this up in order to serve on some obscure government commission set up to consider tariff problems, which does not sound much of an improvement on worrying about the supplies of bandages and bed-pans. For the last two years of the war he was more fruitfully occupied in doing the thing he did best: writing about society instead of trying to run it. He turned his attention once again to the sprawling essays that were to congeal, posthumously, into *Economy and Society*.

After the armistice he embarked upon a political career, almost. He joined the newly formed *Deutsche Demokratische Partei* and allowed his name to go forward on the short list of candidates for a Frankfurt constituency. According to his wife, Marianne, Weber was fairly confident of being adopted as the party's candidate. He did not, in the expected way, bother to canvas for support — either because he thought the result was a foregone conclusion or, more likely, because he could not quite bring himself to descend into the grubby arena of party politics. At all events, he failed to get the nomination; the selection conference passed him over in favour of a local nonentity. Weber was apparently surprised as well as deeply upset by the result. This man who was so astute about the mechanics of power at the level of theory turned out to be somewhat naive when it came to the practicalities of power.

Perhaps his rejection was all to the good. He would have made a terrible politician. Someone of his independent and wayward cast of mind would have found it unbearable to toe the party line or to spout official doctrine. Wisely, if rather sulkily, he turned a deaf ear to the entreaties of his close friends to have another shot at the prize he dearly wanted. As far as politics was concerned, the only kind of greatness he was willing to accept was the kind that would be thrust upon him. As it turned out, none of this mattered; in the late spring of 1920 he caught pneumonia and died. He was 56.

1

Methods and Procedures

Weber's pronouncements on method are commonly drawn upon by those theorists who seek to press a sharp distinction between the aims and procedures of the natural sciences and the aims and procedures of the social sciences. Although this is a line of thought that certainly precedes Weber, it is not too surprising that his teachings should be so frequently used as ammunition by those who oppose the pretensions of 'scientific' social theory. To begin with, no one is more insistent than Weber that the fundamental unit of investigation must always be the individual. This perspective in itself, of course, would not necessarily rule out the kinds of methods and procedures favoured by men in white coats, as the work of behavioural psychologists makes clear. Rather, it is the reason Weber gives for focusing upon the individual and not upon groups or collectivities; namely, that only the individual is capable of 'meaningful' social action. Weber says that it may often be useful, for certain purposes, to treat social groups or aggregates 'as if' they were individual beings. But this is nothing more than an allowable theoretical fiction.[1] As far as the "subjective interpretation of action" is concerned, "collectivities must be treated as *solely* the resultants and

modes of organization of the particular acts of individual persons ..."[2]
His position is summed up as follows:

> for sociological purposes there is no such thing as a collective
> personality which 'acts'. When reference is made in a socio-
> logical context to a state, a nation, a corporation, a family or
> an army corps, or to similar collectivities, what is meant is ...
> only a certain kind of development of actual or possible social
> actions of individual persons.[3]

Collectivities cannot think, feel, perceive; only people can. To
assume otherwise is to impute a spurious reality to what are in effect
conceptual abstractions. Furthermore, because it is the task of social
science to penetrate the subjective understandings of the individual, to
get at the motives for social action, this enterprise is bound to be quite
different from that undertaken by the natural sciences. Weber says that
we do not 'understand' the behaviour of cells or the movement of the
planets. We observe the structure of the cells and the motion of the
stars and then try to formulate general laws about structure and motion.
We, the observers, impose our own explanations upon these phenomena
by the application of our own concepts and categories.

With social behaviour it is all very different. People, unlike mole-
cules or planets, have motives for their actions. Their behaviour is guided
by subjective meanings. What is more, social actors have their own ideas
and explanations as to why they behave in the way that they do, and
these ideas and explanations themselves are an indispensable part of any
comprehensive account of their conduct. It is a fairly safe bet that
falling apples do not have a concept of gravity. Contrast this with, say,
political or religious behaviour. People most certainly do have their own
concepts associated with politics and religion. They employ notions like
'nationalism' and 'class struggle', or 'sin' and 'redemption'. Indeed, their
behaviour is only explicable in the light of such notions. These notions
or concepts enter into the actors' conduct as motivational forces.

Understandably enough, some latter day theorists have con-
cluded from all this that the principal task of sociology is to address
itself directly to the meanings and concepts that enjoy common currency
among the actors themselves, unsullied by the formal constructs of the
observer. Looked at from this angle, the activity of social science is
more akin to that of the philosophy of science than to natural science
proper. The philosophy of science is concerned less with understanding
the physical universe than with understanding the subjective meanings
of scientists themselves as a professional body. It examines the procedures and assumptions, social as well as technical, that inform the

conduct of scientists as actors. It is thus a 'second order' activity because it constructs theories about theories.[4] Sociology, too, is said to be a second order activity in so far as it deals with the theories and conceptions of social actors themselves, and not with their conduct in the raw, as it were. This is precisely the charge often levelled against positivism — that it does seek to make sense of behaviour in the raw by ignoring the motives and subjective states of the actors concerned. Durkheim's sociology stands out as the obvious target.

At any rate, Weber's heavy emphasis on the individual and internal meanings could hardly be in greater contrast to Durkheim's position. For Durkheim, the only unit that really counted for explanatory purposes was the collectivity, and to make individual motives and perceptions the principal object of enquiry would be to forfeit everything of sociological interest. The reason for this was that in the course of their dealings with one another, individuals created a kind of synthesis or social compound, rather in the way that the combination of certain chemicals produces an entirely new compound. It is this synthesis, or emergent property, which is the very stuff of social reality and hence the proper object of enquiry. Since this reality could never be reduced to its constituent parts, it was clearly not accessible via the mental or emotional states of individual actors.

In setting out his case against the individualist perspective Durkheim did not have Weber specifically in mind. Yet his argument does read uncannily like a direct riposte to Weber's recommendation to treat collectivities as the "particular acts of individual persons". If Durkheim had chosen to address his remarks specifically to Weber he would not have had to alter them at all.

Weber's case for taking the individual's subjective meanings as the starting point of social enquiry is spelled out in the course of his advocacy of the method called *Verstehen*. What is meant by this is the attempt to comprehend social action through a kind of empathetic liaison with the actor on the part of the observer. The strategy is for the investigator to try to identify with the actor and his motives and to view the course of conduct through the actor's eyes rather than his own. Weber did not regard *Verstehen* merely as a way of sounding out a person's own account and evaluation of his conduct by way of interviews and the like. He saw it as a method that could be applied to the understanding of historical events, when there was no one left around to interview. We could seek to show why actors followed a certain path of conduct by reconstructing the situational choices and constraints facing them at the time. We are perfectly capable of putting ourselves in someone else's shoes and imagining how we might have acted in similar circumstances. As Weber puts it, "one need not have been Caesar in order to understand Caesar".[5] We can readily make sense of Caesar's actions by seeing them as the working out of an "understandable sequence of motivation".[6]

The argument being canvassed by the *Verstehen* approach is that social actors are always faced with choices. Conduct is not governed by inexorable social forces that propel people in one direction or another. Actors decide to take certain courses of action in preference to others, and their decisions are powerfully affected by their perception of opportunities and constraints. It is therefore necessary, in any given case, to get some understanding of how the options were actually weighed up and assessed. This is an approach which is obviously not too congenial to any school of thought that seeks to uncover some hidden purpose or logic to history. Far from unfolding in accordance with a pre-ordained pattern, history becomes virtually open-ended. Almost anything can happen.

Weber distinguishes between two types of *Verstehen*. These are 'direct observational understanding' (*aktuelles Verstehen*) and 'explanatory understanding' (*erklärendes Verstehen*).[7] He gives as an example of direct observational understanding our ability to grasp the fact that someone is angry simply by reading his facial expression. We experience the same kind of understanding when we observe a woodcutter chopping wood, or a hunter aiming his rifle at an animal. Merely observing these acts is enough to tell us *what* is going on. However, to comprehend *why* it is going on we need to have recourse to explanatory understanding. It is through *erklärendes Verstehen* that we try to grasp the motives and subjective meanings of the various actions. We understand the action of the woodcutter in this second sense once we discover whether he is chopping wood to earn a wage, to build up a supply for his own use, or to work off a fit of temper. Similarly, we arrive at explanatory understanding of the action of the hunter when we learn whether he is killing for food or for sport. Expressed in general terms, we achieve explanatory understanding by placing the act in question in an intelligible "sequence of motivation, the understanding of which can be treated as an explanation of the actual course of behaviour".[8] In other words, we make sense of an act by placing it in a wider context of meaning. It is only by reference to a broader framework of knowledge that any social act can be properly understood and explained.

Weber makes it perfectly plain that the *Verstehen* approach is not to be thought of as the be-all and end-all of social explanation. It has to be supplemented by other techniques of investigation, including the 'scientific' efforts favoured by the positivists.[9] In fact, Weber occasionally seems to look upon *Verstehen* as a fruitful source of hypotheses about behaviour – hypotheses that must then be subjected to empirical scrutiny and validation. And in doing this it is quite in order to bring into play forensic skills and quantitative methods in the classic Durkheimian fashion.

Unlike some of his intellectual heirs, Weber by no means regarded the use of statistical techniques as an exercise in mystification or as a distortion of the subtle realities of social life. Statistical probability was an important check upon the general validity of any proposition. At the same time, caution was called for in attaching explanatory significance to numerical correlations. The fact that two variables showed a consistently high degree of correlation would not in itself suffice to establish a causal connection between them. For causation to be proven it would be necessary to show that the relationship between the variables was intuitively meaningful. If it could be demonstrated that the rise and fall of the pound on the foreign exchange markets exactly paralleled the rise and fall in the divorce rate, we would not be warranted in claiming a causal link between the two events. There is no plausible 'sequence of motivation' that connects actions on the money market with decisions about the fate of marriage. As Weber expresses it,

> If adequacy in respect to meaning is lacking, then no matter how high the degree of uniformity and how precisely its probability can be numerically determined, it is still an incomprehensible statistical probability ... Statistical uniformities constitute understandable types of action, and thus constitute sociological generalizations, only when they can be regarded as manifestations of the understandable subjective meaning of a course of social action.[10]

While statistical correlations may sensitize us to the possibility of a causal link, such a link can only be established if we can satisfy ourselves that there is a connecting sequence of motivations. All this suggests that *Verstehen* is to be understood not as an alternative to positivism and the scientific method, as it is sometimes said to be, but as a corrective against the too mechanical application of this method.[11]

II

Be this as it may, Weber's exposition of *Verstehendesoziologie* raises a number of awkward questions that are left for the most part unanswered.

In the first place, his distinction between two types of *Verstehen* — direct observational understanding and explanatory understanding — is neither helpful nor altogether plausible. It is difficult to see why the direct observation of an act qualifies as any kind of 'understanding' of it at all. If, for example, we were to come across a group of people sitting in a circle with their eyes shut we would not be in much of a position to understand even *what* they were doing. They could be rehearsing a play, communing with the spirits, or getting quietly stoned. Only when we had garnered further information that would enable us to discover the social purpose of their activity, and relate it to some familiar cultural context, would we be in a position to say that we understood it. Weber regards this as the second type of *Verstehen* — explanatory understanding; this is understanding arrived at by placing the act in question in a wider framework of meaning. But surely this is the only one possible type of understanding. Merely observing an act is no kind of understanding whatsoever. We cannot in fact properly comprehend *what* is going on unless we know *why* it is going on.

Weber's own examples can be used to illustrate the point. We can only be said to 'understand' what the woodcutter or the hunter are doing when we find out the reason why one is wielding his axe and the other is aiming his gun. The only real distinction is between merely seeing or observing an action on the one hand, and understanding an action on the other. There are not two types of understanding involved. The oddity of Weber's distinction is made especially apparent by his claim that we can "understand by direct observation . . . the meaning of the proposition $2 \times 2 = 4$ when we hear or read it. This is a case of the direct rational understanding of ideas".[12] But it hardly needs to be said that in order to understand even this simple proposition the observer would need to have at least some background knowledge of the mysteries of arithmetic before these symbols could be invested with meaning. For anyone not equipped with the appropriate cultural framework the sight of these numbers would result not in *aktuelles Verstehen* but blank incomprehension.

There are certain other difficulties about *Verstehen* as a method or procedure that Weber now and then alludes to but never really comes to grips with. One such difficulty is that in order to understand the actor's conduct by way of empathy, it is necessary that the observer should be on roughly the same normative and moral wavelength as the actor. If they have widely divergent outlooks or incompatible beliefs the empathetic connection cannot be fully made. Weber remarks that

... many ultimate ends or values toward which experience shows that human action may be oriented, often cannot be understood completely ... The more radically they differ from our own ultimate values ... the more difficult it is for us to understand them empathically.[13]

This is held to be especially true in the case of deeply held spiritual or political beliefs. Serious obstacles to empathetic understanding would confront observers who were themselves

... not susceptible to unusual acts of religious and charitable zeal, or persons who abhor extreme rationalist fanaticism (such as the fanatic advocacy of the 'rights of man').[14]

A similar point is made by Peter Winch, himself an enthusiast of the Verstehen approach.

[An] historian or sociologist of religion must himself have some religious feeling if he is to make sense of the religious movement he is studying and understand the considerations which govern the lives of its participants.[15]

Weber sometimes goes further than this by suggesting that there is something inherently impenetrable about certain types of religious experience, and that however sympathetic the observer may be to such experiences the very process of trying to explain them leads to a distortion of their meaning.

The religious experience as such is of course irrational ... In its highest, mystical form it is ... distinguished by its aboslute incommunicability. It has a specific character and appears as knowledge, but cannot be adequately reproduced by means of our lingual and conceptual apparatus. It is further true that every religious experience loses some of its content in the attempt at rational formulation, the further the conceptual formulation goes, the more so.[16]

It would seem to follow that any procedure based on Verstehen would be especially difficult to put into practice if actor and observer were from entirely different cultures. The western observer of an exotic tribal society would be seriously impeded in his attempts at understanding because of the wide normative gulf between himself and the subjects of his enquiry. According to Weber, "our ability to share the feelings of primitive men is not very much greater" than our ability to know the "subjective state of mind of an animal ..."[17] This is

quite similar to the thesis put forward by Lévy-Bruhl to the effec
that primitive peoples have a 'pre-logical' mentality that cannot readily
be comprehended by western modes of reasoning and understanding
Although Weber does not himself pursue this point, it squares quite
well with his usual working assumption that rationality is largely a
product of western civilization.

If the subjective meanings of primitive peoples are not accessible
to the trained western observer this would appear to strike a mortal
blow to the discipline of social anthropology. Social anthropology
justifies its existence by the claim that it is perfectly possible to com
prehend the motives and sentiments of people in exotic cultures and to
make them understandable to a western audience. As far as professional
anthropology is concerned, making sense of the beliefs and activities
of tribal man does not require anything like a shared set of values and
assumptions on the part of actor and observer. Durkheim also might
have found Weber's suggestion rather bizarre. After all, his own theory
of religion was based almost entirely upon a close analysis of the
rituals and beliefs of Australian aborigines. Durkheim apparently
encountered no insuperable difficulty in understanding and making
intelligible the 'elementary forms of the religious life' — notwith
standing the rather wide cultural gulf between the aboriginal tribesman
and the Parisian scholar.

Presumably, Weber would be forced to argue that the western
observer, however sensitive and perceptive, could only hope to arrive
at a partial or hazy understanding of tribal society. Durkheim or the
visiting anthropologist would never be able to grasp the full meaning
and significance of religious or secular life as experienced by the actors
themselves. They could offer only a very imperfect version of this
reality since the process of seeing it through western lenses and trans
lating it into western categories of thought and language would neces
sarily distort it.

Now Durkheim and the anthropologist could have a ready rejoinder
to this objection, and it is one that strikes at the very heart of the
Verstehen approach. The rejoinder would be: How could Weber possibly
demonstrate that the western observer had indeed failed in the attempt
to understand fully the subjective meanings and motives of primitive
man? How could Weber show that there really was a discrepancy
between the religious or mystical experiences of tribal people and the
western observer's own rendering of these experiences? For Weber to be
able to show conclusively that the observer had presented a flawed
version of reality, he would have to argue that he, Weber, had managed
to get at the truly authentic version. In which case, either the propo

sition concerning the inscrutability of the primitive mind, and the inaccessibility of religious experience, falls down; or else Weber would have to claim uniquely privileged access to these mysterious depths.

The nagging question that haunts all attempts to adopt a *Verstehen* procedure, even where actor and observer do share the same cultural background, is: How can I be sure that I have in fact grasped and understood the subjective state of the actor? How could I know if I had *mis*understood? Weber's recommendation is that the observer should check his interpretation against some external, behavioural yardstick. But if the actor's conduct is to be the ultimate test of his inner state, it would be just as well to concentrate upon such conduct in the first place and forget about subjective meanings. It seems that the propositions generated by *Verstehen* are either unverifiable, because of the observer's inability to demonstrate the correctness of his empathetic efforts; or they must be ratified by behavioural indices that thereby render his empathetic efforts redundant.

There is also something else slightly worrying about Weber's claim that we are unlikely to be able to make sense of activities and beliefs with which we cannot empathize. Apart from the familiar example of religious behaviour he also mentions political involvement, such as "the fanatic advocacy of the 'rights of man'" — which sounds like Weberese for radical socialism or Marxism.[18] The implication would seem to be that *Verstehendesoziologie* is not applicable to the investigation of values and beliefs which are deeply and passionately held. This is unfortunate in a way, because 'fanatical' commitments of various kinds are generally regarded by sociologists and others as especially intriguing objects of enquiry. If the observer's personal distaste for, or coolness towards, such commitments rendered him unfit to investigate them, the scope of sociology would be considerably reduced. The study of fascism would have to be left to those who sympathized to some extent with the fascist cause; Leninism could only be made sense of by Leninists; and so forth.[19]

It is worth noting that Weber himself never felt in the least constrained by his own emotional distance from the subjects of his enquiry. Although he described himself as 'religiously unmusical' he was perfectly willing to embark upon a series of interpretative studies of Calvinism, Hinduism, Buddhism, Confucianism, Judaism and Islam. In these studies he did not feel it incumbent upon himself to qualify his many statements about religious experience and meaning on the grounds of his own lack of belief. He could quite confidently interpret these religions as if seeing them through the eyes of the faithful. The interpretations resulting from this empathetic exercise are discussed in the following chapter.

III

As a method of enquiry, *Verstehen* would seem to rest on the supposition that individuals are typically aware of their motives for action and of their subjective states in general. If the actor's own meanings and perceptions of reality are an important ingredient in the explanation of conduct, these meanings and perceptions must be treated as social facts in their own right. On the face of it, then, there does not appear to be much room in this approach for anything equivalent to Marx's notion of false consciousness. Marx sought to distinguish true perceptions and understandings from false perceptions and understandings — true ones being those broadly congruent with the individual's class interests. Because of the contaminating influence of bourgeois ideology, the average person's conceptions of social reality tended to be extremely faulty. Consequently, any attempt to view reality as perceived by the actor would be likely to reproduce the false or twisted version of things propagated by the reigning orthodoxy. Since true consciousness or class consciousness operates beneath the surface of everyday life, as a latent rather than a manifest force, it could not be tapped by *Verstehen* procedures.

Since Weber was thoroughly conversant with the Marxist notion of false consciousness he might have been expected to cast some doubt upon it in the course of establishing his own views on method. He could have argued, for example, that the distinction between true and false consciousness was at best unhelpful and at worst invalid. If somebody perceives a situation in a certain way and acts upon the basis of that perception, then for explanatory purposes his way of seeing things must be treated as the relevant social datum. The issue of truth or falsity would not be to the point. What really counts is the actor's own consciousness of reality, however it is construed, since it is this that actually motivates his social conduct. Although this line of argument is one that would have been quite consistent with his doctrinal statements on *Verstehen*, Weber did not in fact adopt it. Paradoxically, he chose instead to advance a point of view that was not too dissimilar from Marx's own. That is to say, he cast grave doubt upon the individual's capacity to comprehend the full significance of his own actions and to grasp their subjective meaning.

> In the great majority of cases actual action goes on in a state
> of inarticulate half-consciousness or actual unconsciousness of
> its subjective meaning. The actor is more likely to 'be aware'
> of it in a vague sense than he is to 'know' what he is doing or
> be explicitly self-conscious about it ... Only occasionally ...
> is the subjective meaning of the action, whether rational or
> irrational, brought clearly into consciousness. The ideal type
> of meaningful action where the meaning is fully conscious
> and explicit is a marginal case.[20]

It will be noted that Weber shies away from using the term 'false consciousness'; but to say that in the ordinary course of events the action of the typical individual is carried out in a state of "inarticulate half-consciousness or actual unconsciousness of its subjective meaning" is not unlike Marx's portrayal of the mind of alienated man. This gloomy assessment of the individual's mental capacities fits more comfortably into the explanatory framework of historical materialism than into *Verstehendesoziologie*. If the actors themselves are not, after all, especially well equipped to know their own motives and to understand their own meanings, what exactly is the use of Weber's method? How could we even begin to make sense of social action through the eyes of the participants if, on Weber's reckoning, the participants themselves have such a myopic view of everything?

Weber's not very helpful piece of advice is that the sociologist should proceed 'as if' actors behaved in a fully meaningful way. By imagining how people would act if they were in full possession of their consciousness, and comparing this with the way that they actually behaved, the sociologist could show the extent of deviation from the path of truly rational action. The success of this procedure would naturally depend on the observer having greater insight into the subjective state of the actor than the actor had himself. To plot the course of deviation someone has to know what the theoretically true course is. Perhaps it was modesty that prevented Weber from declaring outright that the sociologist, unlike the ordinary mortals he studied, was not afflicted by the deformities of consciousness that would make this task impossible.

IV

The comparison between some theoretically postulated 'pure' form of social action and the actual course of social conduct is a procedural device that Weber frequently recommends in his writings on method.

It assumes especial importance in his discussion of ideal-type constructs and their uses. Ideal-types are conceptual abstractions that we employ in trying to get to grips with the complexities of the social world. Weber properly points out that we cannot grasp social phenomena in their totality. Patterns of behaviour and institutional forms like capitalism, or Protestantism, or bureaucracy, are each composed of a large number of interconnected elements, both normative and structural. In order to comprehend any such institution or social formation it is necessary to reduce it to its core components. We do this by singling out and accentuating the central or basic features of the institution in question and suppressing or downgrading those features that could be considered marginal to it. This means that our ideal-type of capitalism, or the bourgeois revolution, or whatever, is unlikely to be an accurate representation of the real thing. It is almost bound to be a somewhat slanted or exaggerated version, rather in the way that a cartoonist's caricature is an exaggerated version of a still recognizable face. Thus, an ideal-type of the bourgeois revolution will not conform exactly to the features of any one particular bourgeois revolution; rather, it will be a kind of distillation of the principal features that are characteristic of these revolution in general. In other words, ideal-types only approximate to social reality, they do not and cannot mirror it faithfully.

Weber acknowledges that the selection of elements that go to make up ideal-types is a somewhat arbitrary affair. What is picked out and accentuated, and what is played down, will to some extent be influenced by the kinds of problem being investigated and the questions being posed. It would thus not make much sense to speak of an ideal-type being correct or incorrect. For one type of enquiry it might be best to select one constellation of elements, for another type of enquiry a quite different set of elements might be more appropriate.

The point that Weber is touching upon here is that it is illusory to imagine that we can somehow capture the 'real essence' of social reality. Social reality does not possess a real essence because it is always capable of being constructed or represented in various different ways. What counts as social reality depends pretty much upon the conceptual apparatus through which we view it in the first place. Weber's stance on this is, again, noticeably different from that of Marx and Durkheim. Marx was inclined to distinguish between the mere appearances of reality and the essence of reality. Surface reality was never quite the same as the deeper, underlying reality. Hence his celebrated dictum that ". . . all science would be superfluous if the outward appearance and the essence of things directly coincided."[21] As far as Marx is concerned there is some ultimate and irreducible level of reality that is not a mere artefact of our own conceptual making. Although there might be different ways of depicting capitalism, the state, and so forth, these different constructs were certainly not to be granted equal validity. There were false constructions and true constructions, bourgeois or ideological conceptions and scientific conceptions.

Durkheim's view is broadly similar. In his analysis of collective behaviour he is not proposing one possible interpretation among others; he is claiming to reveal the very stuff of social life. In reducing religion to its 'elementary forms' he is seeking to lay bare the substance of supernatural belief, the substance that is found in all religions from the simplest to the most complex. Durkheim's standard working assumption is that the quintessential nature of any social phenomenon can be identified by showing what is common to its various manifestations. The task is to uncover what is universal to all religions, to all systems of morality, to all legal institutions, and so on. What is it that apparently disparate things actually share in common? For Durkheim the point of the exercise is not to set up ideal-type constructs that are only weak approximations of social reality, but to penetrate to the fundamental core of reality.

Seen from Weber's angle, even if it were possible to pinpoint some quintessential substance of religion or morality or law, this would still leave all the interesting questions unanswered. In the case of religion, for example, it would still be necessary to show how the doctrinal expressions of the sacred varied from one religion to another. For Durkheim, "The details of dogmas and rites are secondary".[22] For Weber, they are of the utmost importance, since different dogmas motivate very different types of social action. Forget the essence of religion, he implies; let us examine instead the ways in which religions differ in their consequences for social conduct. And the same goes for other complex institutions. Sociological enquiry is more fruitfully directed to the variations that are found within and between institutional forms, rather than to the search for some metaphysical entity that they supposedly share in common. Once the focus shifts to the variety of institutional forms, their types and sub-types, a theoretical device such as the ideal-type is indispensable as a means of bringing some conceptual order to the chaos of reality.

Weber suggests that the ideal-type is to be used as a kind of yardstick against which to compare and evaluate empirical cases. The discrepancies between the ideal-type and the factual forms of the institution or behaviour pattern being investigated thus become the object of theoretical interest. The aim is to show the nature and extent of variation between our ideal-type of, say, bureaucracy or the messianic sect, and particular cases of these phenomena. It is clear that Weber regards this procedure as a necessary prelude to causal explanation.

> Whatever the content of the ideal-type ... it has only one function in an empirical investigation. Its function is the comparison with empirical reality in order to establish its divergencies or similarities ... and to understand and explain them causally.[23]

However, Weber never really makes clear what kind of explanatory pay-off this procedure actually yields. Merely to show that there is indeed a lack of correspondence between ideal-type and empirical reality is not a discovery guaranteed to set the pulse racing. In the first place, there is almost bound to be such lack of fit, given the way that ideal-types are constructed. If we are required to select a few key components from among the possible range of components, and to give these what Weber calls a "one-sided accentuation",[24] then it follows that almost any empirical case will diverge from the pure type. Moreover, it is by no means obvious what possible *causal* inferences could be drawn from this fact. Indeed, the very notion of causality seems out of place here. Any divergences between ideal-type and reality are a direct function of the manner in which the ideal-type was originally constructed. Had we chosen to select and emphasize a different set of elements we should have discovered a different set of discrepancies. How could we be sure that the discrepancies we found were not 'caused' simply by the sloppiness of our original construct?

V

Weber points out that ideal-types are, of necessity, morally loaded constructs. "All knowledge of cultural reality ... is always knowledge from *particular points of view*".[25] There can be no such thing as an

> ... absolutely 'objective' scientific analysis of culture or ... of 'social phenomena' independent of special and 'one-sided' viewpoints according to which — expressly or tacitly, consciously or unconsciously — they are selected, analyzed and organized for expository purposes.[26]

Weber drives home the point that social reality cannot be apprehended by letting the facts 'speak for themselves'. Social facts do not exist as things in their own right, waiting to be gathered up like pebbles

Criticism of Durkheim

interpretation

on a beach. What counts as a social fact is very much determined by the moral spectacles through which we view the world. Weber is scathingly dismissive of those theorists who urge us to evacuate our minds of all presuppositions in order that we might perceive social reality in all its purity. This was a doctrine that even Durkheim, of all people, occasionally espoused. In his own treatise on method, Durkheim says that when investigating social life "All preconceptions must be eradicated. [This is] ... the basis of all scientific method."[27] His repeated emphasis on the need to treat social facts as 'things' also implies a sturdy, no-nonsense approach to the problem.

For Weber, on the other hand, since the eradication of all preconceptions was not humanly possible, the social construction of facts was extremely problematic. Because social facts only existed by virtue of the concepts employed to define and organize them, we could in effect bring new facts into being and dispose of others simply by altering our conceptual frame of reference. Entities like social classes, for example, could be abolished at a single conceptual stroke. Now you see them, now you don't.

Weber's insistence that all theoretical constructs are shot through with biases of one kind or another is not easy to reconcile with the explanatory claims he makes on behalf of ideal-types. Since it is possible to construct quite different ideal-types of the same phenomenon, there is an initial problem of how to decide between them. On what grounds could we conclude that one carried greater explanatory weight than another? The natural temptation would be to say that the matter could be settled by exposing them to the test of the factual world and comparing their performance. But since for Weber such a factual world does not exist independently of the constructs through which we view it, a straightforward comparison is not really possible. Each ideal-type would simply feed upon those social facts of its own making.[28]

Suppose, for example, we wished to construct an ideal type of 'democracy'. One possibility would be to highlight features such as free elections, competing political parties, legal right of opposition, the separation of powers, and the guarantee of civil liberties. Using this as our ideal-type of democracy, we would find that communist or socialist systems diverged considerably from it. Western political systems, by contrast, would show a much closer approximation to it. On that basis, we could conclude that western capitalist systems were more democratic than socialist systems. However, it would be quite feasible to construct an ideal-type of democracy that gave one-sided emphasis to a different set of criteria. The key features could be regarded

as the absence of a property-owning or exploiting class, and the absence
of those gross inequalities of wealth that effectively concentrate power
in the hands of the few at the expense of the many, notwithstanding
the latter's purely formal liberties and rights. Measured against this
conceptual yardstick, western capitalist states would tend to show
greater divergence from the pure type than many socialist states.
Socialist states could thus be judged more democratic. Because both
constructs are morally slanted, and inevitably so, it is hard to see how
either of them could claim explanatory superiority over the other. This
is the problem with all ideal-types. Hence, not everyone will endorse
Weber's enthusiastic claim that these constructs

> are of great value for research and of high systematic value
> for expository purposes when they are used as conceptual
> instruments for *comparison* with and the *measurement* of
> reality.[29]

It is at least arguable that ideal-types tell us less about social reality
than about the inbuilt preconceptions of the investigator. Weber
virtually says this much himself. To pit one version of reality against
another involves, ultimately, a conflict of moralities.

> It must be recognized that general views of life and the universe
> can never be the products of increasing empirical knowledge,
> and that the highest ideals, which move us most forcefully,
> are always formed only in the struggle with other ideals
> which are just as sacred to others as ours are to us.[30]

This being the case, Weber would not seem to be the most likely
candidate to champion the cause of 'value-free' social theory. How
could sociology ever attain neutrality if its operational tools were
saturated with the observer's own values and preconceptions? Given his
views on the status of knowledge as an inescapably social and moral
construct, it is at first blush puzzling that Weber should have raised
such loud and insistent demands for the exclusion of value-judgements
from sociological observations.

The puzzle is only partly resolved when it becomes apparent that
Weber's demands on this score were rather modest and limited in scope.
All he really asked was that scholars should refrain from openly proclaiming their personal views on matters of social fact. It was the duty
of the teacher or the scholar to set out the evidence for income distribution or the incidence of strikes without regarding the evidence as a
cause for lamentation or rejoicing. The classroom was not to be used as

a platform for making thinly-veiled political speeches or for engaging in any kind of tub-thumping. It was an

> intrinsically simple demand that the investigator and teacher should keep unconditionally separate the establishment of empirical facts . . . and his own practical evaluations . . .[31]

The question Weber never really faced up to was whether ethical neutrality could be violated unwittingly, despite the sociologist's willingness to abstain from openly proclaiming his own views. His belief in the capacity of social scientists to "distinguish between empirical knowledge and value judgements"[32] is not dissimilar to the belief of newspaper editors in their capacity to distinguish between news and comment. In presenting the news they stick scrupulously to the facts, recording events without bias or favour. Judgement on the facts is reserved for the editorial columns. However, there now appears to be a small army of sociologists — the 'media theorists' — whose principal activity is to pour cold water on this notion. They tell us that what counts as 'news' is in fact the end product of a very selective social process. In recording some events and suppressing others, as well as in the moral vocabulary employed in the manufacture of news, certain biases and preconceptions are quietly at work. What purports to be an impartial recitation of factual events is thus a thoroughly loaded presentation. The biases may operate in a more subtle and subterranean fashion than they do in the case of editorial comment, but that makes them all the more effective.[33]

A similar charge could be made against social research. Merely because the investigator refrained from openly ranting or moralizing about his findings would not thereby make them value-free. The working assumptions that guided the research, and the choice of concepts employed, would ensure that the final product had a certain moral coloring. For reasons already alluded to, this might be especially so if ideal-types were used. Weber offers no guidance on how it would be possible to arrive at value-free results with the aid of these constructs.

He would have been on somewhat firmer ground if he had not conflated value-judgements with partisanship. He could have conceded that since all forms of social enquiry entail the use of concepts and constructs that are morally tinted, the research product could not possibly be value-free. At the same time, he could quite reasonably have sustained his case against partisanship in the lecture room and in academic publications. The sociologist cannot, try as he may, avoid making value judgements in his work. But he *can* avoid spouting his own tedious opinions on this and that. The fact that implicit evaluations cannot be expunged from social enquiry is no warrant for giving a completely free rein to the soap-box brigade.

VI

Although he extols the explanatory virtues of the ideal-type, Weber does not generally apply it in accordance with the recommended usage. His construct of bureaucracy, perhaps the most influential of his formulations, provides an illustration. The first step, that of setting up the ideal-type, is carried out in exemplary fashion. That is, Weber selects out and emphasizes the features of bureaucracy that he takes to be its distinctive hallmark. Among these features are: a formal hierarchy of rank and officialdom, the application of rules according to the book, promotion by merit or seniority, strict control of the files and information, and so on. These elements, Weber suggests, combine to endow bureaucracy with a "*technical* superiority over any other form of organization."

> The fully developed bureaucratic apparatus compares with other organizations exactly as does the machine with the non-mechanical modes of production. Precision, speed, unambiguity, knowledge of files, continuity, discretion, unity, strict subordination, reduction of friction and of material and personal costs — these are raised to the optimum point in the strictly bureaucratic administration.[34]

Having set up his ideal-type bureaucracy, Weber might have been expected to compare it against empirical cases of bureaucracy. He could have used it as an evaluative yardstick for examining the administrative practices of, say, the Prussian civil service, or the university bureaucracy, or German trade unions. He could have proposed, as a working hypothesis, that the greater the divergence between these or similar bureaucracies and the ideal-type, the greater their loss of 'technical superiority' in administrative affairs. But Weber does none of these things. He presents no evidence to show that organizations which depart from the ideal-type do in fact suffer from a loss of precision, speed and unambiguity, or from an increase in friction and material and personal costs. The technical superiority of bureaucracy is simply stated as an axiomatic truth that requires no empirical proof.

It is worth noting, too, that Weber presents bureaucracy as a system governed by highly formalized and inflexible rules. It is an administrative arrangement in which personal volition, feeling or sentiments can have no place.

> Bureaucracy develops the more perfectly the more it is 'de-humanized', the more completely it succeeds in eliminating from official business love, hatred, and all purely personal, irrational, and emotional elements which escape calculation.[35]

Bureaucratic conduct is governed by a strict regime of regulation and discipline. If all the present incumbents were cast out and replaced by an entirely new set of officials, the system would continue as before. The question thus arises, if bureaucracy can be understood in this way, without paying undue attention to the motives and sentiments of the people who run the show, what becomes of the *Verstehen* approach? On Weber's account, the behaviour of bureaucrats is fashioned by the internal logic of the administrative machine, not by the subjective meanings and perceptions of the actors. Personal motives and subjective meanings appear to be no more relevant to the conduct of Weber's typical bureaucrat than they are to the conduct of Marx's typical capitalist.

This holds true not only for bureaucratic behaviour but for any form of behaviour viewed through the aperture of ideal-types. In singling out those features of an institution that are deemed to be its most typical or characteristic, it follows that atypical or eccentric features are played down. The point about these latter features, that are screened out of the ideal-type, is that they are often likely to be the product of human quirks and idiosyncracies. Ideal-types encourage us to think about institutions and behaviour in a way that can be generalized about rather than particularized. In constructing an ideal-type of the industrial firm, or the nuclear family, the revolutionary sect, or whatever, the aim is to characterize the institution concerned more or less independently of the variety of motives and sentiments of the people who comprise it. The ideal-type, in other words, tends to direct our attention away from individual actors and their perceptions which are the very subject matter of *Verstehendesoziologie.*

This is not, of course, to say that the use of ideal-type constructs and the *Verstehen* approach are necessarily incompatible. Weber himself did not attempt to reconcile or combine them in any of his substantive studies. Indeed, he never even discusses them together in the same breath. However, some of his followers have done so, and with interesting results. Among the most notable examples are the case studies of bureaucracy, most of which have shown it to be an extremely blunt instrument of administration. Real bureaucracies, far from living up to Weber's model of 'precision, speed and unambiguity' are more likely to be cumbersome, slow and full of muddle. Weber tended to highlight the positive functions of the system and to ignore its dysfunctions, whereas most of the recent studies dwell at length upon the things that go wrong.[36] It appears that many of the spanners found in the works are dropped by the flawed human beings who run the system. Bureaucrats, it transpires, rarely behave in the dispassionate and mechanical manner formally required of them. Their conduct is more than a little influenced by personal rivalries, petty squabbles, and a flourishing emotional life among the filing cabinets.

Once the individual incumbents are brought into the picture, and their personal motives, meanings and perceptions are given due attention, we get a clearer understanding of why bureaucracies do not closely correspond to the pure type. Within the formal structure of any bureaucracy there nestles an informal structure designed to meet the personal aims and needs of the staff, and which may often cause the machinery of administration to operate at less than optimum capacity. If Weber had adopted his own *Verstehen* procedure he would have been made aware of this informal structure and would have thus been in a position to explain why discrepancies would be expected to occur between the ideal-type and empirical reality.

It should be said that Weber was certainly no stranger to the idea that people are always likely to depart from any ideal-typical construct of behaviour on personal or emotional grounds. He held, in fact, the rather peculiar view that it was in principle possible for the sociologist to work out what a purely rational course of action would be, for any given situation, on the assumption that the people involved were not influenced by feelings and emotions or similar 'irrational' factors. The extent to which real behaviour departed from this path of pure rationality could then be taken as a measure of the intrusion of irrational elements like anger, pride, jealousy, and so on.

> For the purposes of a typological scientific analysis it is convenient to treat all irrational, affectually determined elements of behaviour as factors of deviation from a conceptually pure type of rational action. For example a panic on the Stock Exchange can be most conveniently analysed by attempting to determine first what the course of action would have been if it had not been influenced by irrational affects; it is then possible to introduce the irrational components as accounting for the observed deviation from this hypothetical course ... The construction of a purely rational

course of action in such cases serves the sociologist as
(ideal type) which has the merit of clear understandabili
lack of ambiguity. By comparison with this it is possit
understand the ways in which actual action is influenced by
irrational factors of all sorts, such as affects and errors, in that
they account for the deviation from the line of conduct which
would be expected on the hypothesis that the action were
purely rational.[37]

If rational conduct is defined as conduct untouched by sentiments,
feelings, and the like, then only robots could possibly attain it. Moreover, it is hard to imagine that the sociologist or anyone else would
really be able to plot the course that action would take in the absence
of emotional and other human distortions. The implication seems to be
that under conditions of pure rationality only one inexorable course
of action would be possible. If more than one line of conduct was
consistent with the demands of rationality, there would be no way of
knowing which of them to adopt as the evaluative base line. Unfortu-
nately, Weber offers no illustration of this pure type of action. We are
left completely in the dark as to how his stockbroker would perform
in a financial crisis if he were not made of flesh and blood. Perhaps by
refusing to 'panic' he would be left with utterly worthless shares on
his hands. Weber's totally rational man looks rather as though he would
be bereft of all those intuitions and sensibilities he would need to pick
his way through the minefield of personal relations.

VII

Before concluding this discussion of Weber's procedural rules, something should be said about his teachings on method in historical ex-
plananion. He wished to set down certain formal procedures that
would enable the investigator to unravel the main threads of causation
in history. Great historical events such as wars and revolutions were
obviously brought about by a combination of many different factors
or antecedents. Nevertheless it could not be assumed that all factors
were of equal importance in bringing about the result. Some were more
instrumental than others. What was called for, therefore, was a systematic procedure by which it would be possible to assess the causal significance of the various factors involved.

The procedure that Weber recommended took the shape of an
imaginative experiment. This required the investigator to weigh up

the probability or likelihood that the historical event in question would still have occurred in the absence of any particular antecedent factor. He would have to ask, for example, whether the First World War would still have happened if the Archduke Ferdinand had not been assassinated; or whether the Bolshevik revolution would still have taken place if Lenin had not been on the scene. If, on the basis of his hypothetical reconstruction, the observer were to conclude that in the absence of these two specific events the 1914 war and the 1917 revolution would *not* have occurred, then these antecedent factors would have to be accorded primary causal significance. If, on the other hand, he were to conclude that the war or the revolution would probably have taken place anyway, even in the absence of these particular events, then their causal contribution would be downgraded accordingly.

What Weber is getting at here is the need to distinguish between two different patterns of causation. The first is where the great event in question would most likely have taken place in the absence of any one particular antecedent factor. The second is where one specific factor was of decisive importance, so that in the absence of that one occurrence the course of history would probably have been quite different. Weber calls the first *adequate* causation, and the second *chance* causation.[38]

Adequate causation applies where the cumulative build-up of social and political tensions has reached such an explosive pitch that any one of a number of quite different critical events could provide the spark needed to set off the powder keg. Thus, even if the Archduke had not been assassinated, the tense political situation in Europe at the time might lead us to suppose that some other major 'incident' would have produced a similar result. *Chance* causation, on the other hand, applies where the social explosion is caused by one unique spark, a factor or event for which there was no substitute. An example of this would be Trotsky's assessment of Lenin's role in the October revolution. According to Trotsky, if Lenin had not been present to take personal charge of events there would have been no revolution. To 'think away' Lenin is to posit a very different outcome to Russian history.[39]

Weber did not wish his method to be understood as an invitation to indulge in fanciful speculation about what might have happened in history if only so-and-so had not occurred. The point of the exercise was to assign different degrees of causal significance to the various ingredients that went into the overall mix, an assessment that could only be made in terms of the balance of probabilities. This task was

made a good deal easier if comparative evidence could be d
If some factors could be treated as constant across a range o
situations, while others could be treated as variable, causal sig   ance
could be more convincingly established. This is one of the strategies
that Weber adopts in weighing up the influence to be attached to
certain religious beliefs in fostering the rise of western capitalism. His
investigation of this large problem drew also upon some of the other
methods and procedures discussed above, with what results we may
now consider.

2

Beliefs and Social Action

I

Weber is often thought of as a theorist who championed the cause of normative explanations in opposition to the claims of historical materialism. He is presented to us as someone who places a heavy accent on the independent role of ideas in social life. Whereas Marx treated values and beliefs as by-products of class or material interests, Weber sought to show that the path of causation often ran in the reverse direction. In fact, though, Weber had quite strong materialist leanings of his own. In his political writings, in particular, he generally discounts the possibility that values or ideology could make much of an imprint upon the hard realities of social structure, especially once it had reached the bureaucratic stage. And even in his writings on religion, where any lurking 'idealist' predilections could be expected to come to the fore, he always maintains that beliefs are effective only within a circumscribed range of what Durkheim would have called 'external social facts'.

Weber's unwarranted reputation as an anti-materialist stems largely from his essays on early Protestantism. His attempt in these essays to demonstrate a link between certain religious precepts and a capitalist

mentality was often transformed into the bowdlerized thesis that
Calvinism was the principal cause of capitalism. That his argument
could be reduced to this simple and dramatic formula, by critics and
admirers alike, was not entirely due to the mental deficiencies of his
readers. The case he presents is replete with ambiguities, inconsisten-
cies, and other intellectual curiosities. It is not therefore surprising that
it should be such a fertile source of those misunderstandings and
quarrelsome exchanges that are the bread and butter of academic life.
Even so, some misunderstandings are less forgiveable than others, and
Weber was entitled to be grumpy about those people who paraphrased
his argument to mean the very opposite of what he actually said. Let
us examine what he said and what it could possibly mean.

In his essays on early Protestantism, Weber set out to explore the
relationship between a particular religious ethic and a certain kind of
capitalist spirit or mentality. It is necessary to speak of a 'certain kind'
of capitalist spirit because Weber identified several different types.
More correctly, he identified several different types of capitalism, each
of which could be presumed to have its own appropriate spirit. Among
the most important of these were *booty capitalism, pariah capitalism,
traditional capitalism,* and *rational capitalism.* [1]

Booty capitalism was a manner of acquiring wealth and riches by
way of war, plunder, and speculative adventures; the archetypal representatives of booty capitalism would be the 'robber barons'. *Pariah
capitalism* was commercial activity, especially money-lending, that was
carried on by social groups excluded from the mainstream of society.
Weber generally regards the Jews as the exemplars of pariah capitalism.
Traditional capitalism was the type of large-scale undertaking found in
all civilizations from the earliest times. These undertakings were usually
set up for specific and limited ends, rather than for the continuous
accumulation of wealth and profit. Finally, *rational capitalism* was a
form of economic activity geared to a regular market, the use of book-
keeping to ensure strict calculability, and the systematic pursuit of
profit by legal means. Above all, rational capitalism entailed the employment of formally free labour and hence the creation of a proletarian
class. It is this variety of capitalism with which we are most familiar
today and which is synonymous with modern capitalism. It is this with
which Weber is almost exclusively concerned.

The reason for this is that rational capitalism originates, uniquely,
in the West. All the other types of capitalism are found independently
in various parts of the globe and in different historical periods. The
rational variety clearly requires very special circumstances to bring it

into being. It was to the elucidation of these special circumstances
that Weber's intellectual energies were directed.

He begins by distinguishing two separate sets of circumstances or
preconditions for the emergence of rational capitalism, the normative
and the institutional. Before this type of economic system can make its
appearance both the rational 'spirit' and the material 'substance' of
capitalism must be present. Each can occur independently of the other
and it is only the fortuitous combination of the two that produces
the revolutionary synthesis. If either one is absent, rational capitalism
has no chance.

Weber's insistence that normative and institutional preconditions —
spirit and substance — can vary independently, produces in effect four
possible combinations:

	Spirit	Substance
(a)	—	—
(b)	—	+
(c)	+	—
(d)	+	+

Case (a) refers to the condition where neither the normative nor
the institutional supports for capitalism are present. Tribal society
would be the obvious example.

In case (b) the institutional preconditions for capitalism are present,
but not the rational economic spirit. This is how Weber often charac-
terizes the situation in Oriental societies. The material infrastructure
of these societies was well suited for capitalist exploitation, but it was
never galvanized into motion by the necessary motivational touch.

Case (c) illustrates the very opposite condition. Here the capitalist
spirit is alive and flourishing, but lacks the proper institutional supports.
As an example of this fairly unusual state of affairs, Weber invites us to
consider the case of Benjamin Franklin, the highest embodiment of
the capitalist spirit, scratching about in the unpromising backwoods
of Pennsylvania.

Case (d) is where spirit and substance coincide to produce the
explosive mix that transforms the basis of economic and social life
and brings modern capitalism into being.

Because Weber regards the normative and institutional prerequisites
of modern capitalism as independent things, he naturally seeks to give a
separate account of each of them. Most of the controversy has centred
upon his account of the origins of the capitalist spirit, so it might be as
well to consider this first.

II

In his discussion of the link between early Protestant or Calvinist beliefs and the rational capitalist mentality, Weber tends to shift back and forth between two rather different lines of argument — what might be called a strong thesis and a weak thesis. The strong thesis is that Calvinist teachings were an active, determinate force in the creation of the capitalist spirit. They were the inspirational drive behind the ideas and practices of rational economic activity. Weber noted that this type of activity was far commoner among the early Protestants than among contemporary Catholics, leading him to declare that "the principal explanation of this difference must be sought in the permanent intrinsic character of their religious beliefs", rather than in their different social circumstances.[2]

The strong thesis proposes that the distinctive ethic of early Protestantism was not merely historically prior to the capitalist spirit but that it was the decisive force in shaping this spirit. In particular, rational economic conduct based on the idea of the 'calling', which Weber regarded as "one of the fundamental elements of the spirit of capitalism . . . was born . . . from the spirit of Christian asceticism"[3] There are many other statements dotted throughout Weber's work that make the same point concerning a direct causal link between the Protestant ethic and the capitalist mentality.

Side by side with this strong thesis runs a weaker one. This claims not that Calvinist ethics actively gave rise to the spirit of capitalism, but only that the two outlooks were in close harmony with each other. The moral code of the typical early Protestant and the economic code of the typical rational capitalist showed an unusual degree of congruence. Baxter the preacher and Franklin the capitalist were unknowingly brothers under the skin. The more cautious approach of the weak thesis is summarized by Weber as follows:

> In view of the tremendous confusion of interdependent influences between the material basis, the forms of social and political organization, and the ideas current in the time of the Reformation, we can only proceed by investigating whether and at what points certain correlations between forms of religious belief and practical ethics can be worked out.[4]

The proposition now is that the capitalist spirit can be shown to have a special affinity with the Protestant ethic, but not that it was 'born' from it. Expressed in this way, it would seem to be an open question as to whether the capitalist spirit could have originated from a source other than early Protestantism. This is one of the many points on which Weber seems to take issue with himself. He dismisses rather crossly any suggestion that the capitalist spirit could only have arisen as a consequence of Calvinism; this is "a foolish and doctrinaire thesis".[5] Yet much of his work on comparative religion seems to be dedicated to establishing this very point.

In his studies of the world religions, Weber seeks to show the manner in which these belief systems act as impediments to the growth of a rational economic outlook. Hinduism, Buddhism, Islam, Confucianism, and medieval Catholicism are all religions which, each in their different ways, are said to be saturated with 'magical' beliefs and rituals that run directly counter to rational economic conduct. Calvinism and its offshoots stands out as the striking exception. This is one of the very few religions devoid of magic and similar encumbrances to the capitalist spirit. The role of Calvinism in the weak thesis is thus something of a passive one. Its decisive importance lies not in what it actively does but in what it does *not* do. It does not stifle the rational acquisitive spirit; and in that respect it is virtually unique. However 'doctrinaire and foolish' it may be to say that no other religion could have performed this feat, the fact of the matter is that Weber is remarkably silent about the likely alternatives.

Although he draws upon both the strong and the weak theses at various points in his presentation, it is probably fair to say that Weber's main inclination is towards the former. Despite all his customary qualifications and caveats, he is undoubtedly concerned to show that early Protestant beliefs made an unparalleled impact upon the conduct of economic life. The various links in his complex chain of reasoning are worth considering in some detail.

III

His starting point is the Calvinist doctrine of predestination. This was the belief that God had decided every person's ultimate fate even while he or she was still in the womb. At the very moment of birth the individual was already earmarked for salvation or damnation, and however dutifully or otherwise he might conduct himself through life made not the slightest difference to the outcome. God's decision was irreversible. As Weber says, the logical consequence of such a belief would seem to be an attitude of fatalism, complete resignation to one's lot. How, then, could the doctrine of predestination be squared with the Calvinists' extremely active economic and social life, and their obsession with the need to perform good works?

Weber's answer is that they were plagued by 'salvation anxiety'. Because Calvinists laboured under the intolerable psychological burden of not knowing whether they had been elected for salvation they were gradually driven to seek signs or proof of grace. Each believer sought to convince himself and others that he was one of the chosen. And for this purpose the most telling kind of activity was that which yielded visible fruits and tangible evidence. As Weber puts it, "faith had to be proved by its objective results in order to provide a firm foundation ..." for the certainty of salvation.[6] The performance of good works consequently became the practical means by which the true believer could discover his state of grace and his final destination.

> Thus, however useless good works might be as a means of attaining salvation ... they are indispensable as a sign of election. They are the technical means, not of purchasing salvation, but of getting rid of the fear of damnation ... In practice this means that God helps those who help themselves. Thus the Calvinist, as it is sometimes put, himself creates his own salvation, or, as would be more correct, the conviction of it.[7]

Salvation anxiety thereby transforms the doctrine of predestination from a potentially fatalistic and passive stance towards the world into an extremely active and busy one. The Calvinist is set upon a course of restless labour and methodical worldly activity as a means of putting to flight internal spiritual doubts. It is the worry about salvation that proves to be the first link in the chain of causation between the Protestant ethic and the spirit of capitalism.

Now this notion of salvation anxiety, which is clearly so important to Weber's argument, raises a number of awkward questions. In the first place, Weber does not exactly bombard us with evidence to show that the typical Calvinist was in fact deeply troubled by uncertainties about salvation. This is a perfectly plausible hunch or inference on Weber's part, but that is not quite the same thing. Neither in the main body of the text of *The Protestant Ethic and the Spirit of Capitalism*, nor in the many miniature essays that masquerade as footnotes to it, is there a record of any statement by a Calvinist layman to support the hypothesis of salvation anxiety. All Weber's citations on the subject are taken from the writings of theologians or preachers, especially the Puritan divines. Weber is asking us to accept that the recorded teachings and pronouncements of religious officials be treated as admissible evidence of the beliefs and practices of ordinary laymen.

We might, of course, be reluctant to swallow this dubious line of argument; but in case we were not, Weber is only too ready to encourage our resistance. In his *General Economic History* he underlines the need to distinguish between the official teachings of religion and the actual practices to which they give rise. In particular, it is "necessary to distinguish between the virtuoso religion of adepts and the religion of the masses".[8] And even in the essays on the Protestant ethic, where he relies so heavily on virtuoso religion, the warning is repeated: "What a religion has sought after as an ideal, and what the actual result of its influence on the lives of its adherents has been, must be sharply distinguished . . ."[9]

Weber might have defended his procedure by claiming that the distinction between the virtuoso religion of adepts and the religion of the masses was not really applicable in the case of early Protestantism. Because there was no priestly hierarchy or church bureaucracy the sermons of the Puritan divines could be taken as fairly accurate reflections of the sentiments of their congregation. Baxter the preacher could thus be regarded as a reliable mouthpiece of the ordinary believer. At any rate, Weber seems to have harboured few doubts that the teachings emanating from the pulpit would be duly absorbed and acted upon by the laity.

Had Weber followed his own recommendations on method he might have enquired into the extent to which common-or-garden Calvinists did indeed share the same beliefs as the divines. Whether or not salvation anxiety was a typical and widespread response to the doctrine of predestination was surely the kind of question that the *Verstehen* approach was meant to raise. Instead of simply imputing a salvation anxiety to the average Calvinist, Weber could have asked how the matter was conceived of and dealt with by the actors themselves. Presumably, the appropriate research strategy would have been to examine the diaries and correspondence and other personal documents of these highly literate people.

On the basis of this kind of evidence it might have been possible to offer at least some rough assessment of just how typical Baxter actually was. In any case, wasn't that supposed to be the whole point of using ideal-type constructs — to compare and evaluate empirical reality against the yardstick of theoretical abstraction? But that is not how Weber proceeds. Baxter's pronouncements are never treated as a purely provisional representation of a religious world-view, a provisional representation that could be modified in the light of further investigation. As far as Weber is concerned, Baxter's utterances *are* the distillation of the Protestant ethic.

It can readily be conceded that a *Verstehen* approach to this problem would have encountered formidable difficulties, not least in the way of documentary sources. Interestingly enough, Weber drops a hint to suggest that such sources were available in enough sufficiency to make the task feasible. He refers to the "fascinating task of presenting the characteristics of ascetic Protestanism through the medium of the biographical literature."[10] The reason he offers for not embarking on this fascinating task is that it would fall outside the limits of his study. It is instructive to learn that evidence bearing upon the popular conception of religion falls outside the scope of a study designed to show the link between beliefs and common social action.

In lieu of evidence of a widespread salvation anxiety, Weber resorts to empathetic understanding. Since it is not necessary to be Caesar in order to understand Caesar, the same no doubt applies to Calvinists. At an important stage in his argument, Weber seems to imagine himself in the position of a true believer faced with the doctrine of predestination.

> For us the decisive problem is: How was this doctrine borne in an age to which the after-life was not only more important, but in many ways also more certain, than all the interests of life in this world? The question, Am I one of the elect? must sooner or later have arisen for every believer and have forced all other interests into the background.[11]

For Weber, it is clearly inconceivable that anyone could live at ease with the uncertainty of predestination. Putting himself in Calvinist shoes he discovers an intense psychological pressure to know the score on salvation, one way or the other. Hence, this is how it must have been for the "broad mass of ordinary men". Their need to know their ultimate fate "necessarily became of absolutely dominant importance."[12]

It is certainly of dominant importance to Weber's thesis that they should have reacted in this way. The manner in which such anxiety was dealt with provides the next vital link in the chain of causation. In order to assuage his troubled mind, the Calvinist busied himself with the performance of good works and worldly activities, the fruits of which could be taken as a sign or proof of election. It was this energetic response to salvation anxiety that set the Calvinist on the uphill path that led to rational economic action.

Let us assume, for argument's sake, that the first link in Weber's chain of reasoning proved to be sound, and that the doctrine of predestination did generally provoke the kind of insecurity that he himself might have felt. Granting all this, would it still necessarily follow that true believers would be *bound* to respond in the manner suggested by Weber? Apparently not, because alternative courses of action were open to them. The most important alternative was not merely a theoretical possibility; it was a moral injunction. The faithful were enjoined to believe that they had been elected for salvation; even to contemplate that it might be otherwise would be a most ungodly thing. As Weber himself acknowledges, even Baxter taught that it was "an absolute duty to consider oneself chosen, and to combat all doubts as temptations of the devil . . ."[13]

This being so, it is not easy to see why Calvinists *must* have been propelled into frantic activity designed to establish proof of election. Any believer who felt the first illicit stirrings of salvation anxiety could simply take comfort in the presumption of election, just as his religion required him to do. To embark upon a relentless search for proof of grace would look very much like the action of a doubter rather than a believer. It seems that Weber's typical Calvinist cannot bring himself to accept the presumption of salvation, and must instead suffer the anguish that only rational worldly activity can mollify. Merely to accept that he was one of the chosen might cause him a good deal less worry, but he would not then be fitted to fulfill the historic role that Weber has sketched out for him.

Having set his typical Calvinist in motion, Weber proceeds to show the manner in which the need to establish proof of salvation led unwittingly to the cultivation of a capitalist spirit. Here the associated notions of 'salvation by works' and the 'calling' assumed particular importance. In embarking upon a life dedicated to the performance of good works the Calvinist brought an unprecedented degree of system and planfulness into social and economic affairs. Weber contrasts the Calvinist way of doing things with "the everday life of an average Christian of the Middle Ages."[14]

> The difference may well be formulated as follows: the normal medieval Catholic layman lived ethically so to speak, from hand to mouth. In the first place he conscientiously fulfilled his traditional duties. But beyond that minimum his good works did not necessarily form a connected, or at least not a rationalized, system of life, but rather remained a succession of individual acts . . .

> The God of Calvinism [by contrast] demanded of his believers not single good works, but a life of good works combined into a unified system . . . The moral conduct of the average

man was thus deprived of its planless and unsystematic character and subjected to a consistent method for conduct as a whole.[15]

By replacing the sloppy and disorganized way of life fostered by Catholic traditionalism with a more rigorous and systematic approach, Calvinism sowed the seeds of rational action that would eventually flower into the capitalist spirit.

Activity in pursuit of one's calling contributed to the same end. As originally taught by Luther, the idea of the calling was that the highest expression of Christian morality came not through monastic asceticism and withdrawal, but in the fulfilment of obligations incumbent upon each person according to his station in life. Luther's conception of the calling, as portrayed by Weber, remained thoroughly conservative and traditionalistic. Each person was bound to follow the calling in which God had seen fit to place him; obedience to authority and endorsement of the status quo were marks of virtue. It was thus "impossible for Luther to establish a new or in any way fundamental connection between worldly activity and religious principles."[16] In a nutshell, "Luther cannot be claimed for the spirit of capitalism . . ."[17]

With Calvinism all this changes. The Calvinist is enjoined to labour diligently and systematically in a calling, but there is no doctrinal insistence on his remaining in the station into which he was born. Indeed, not to seize opportunities for self-improvement would be to squander the gifts bestowed by God and to be found wanting in the proper conduct of His ministry on earth.

Given the general drift of his strong thesis, it follows naturally enough that Weber should construe the significance of the calling and good works as motive forces for economic activity. The implication is that the Calvinist finds release from the fear of damnation by becoming successful in his workaday affairs. To prosper in the marketplace, to flourish in the business world, would seem to be the most tangible evidence of being in God's favour.

> The increase of his profits and possessions was a conspicuous sign of God's blessing. Above all, his worth could be assessed in the eyes of men and of God through success in his calling, provided it was achieved by legal means. God had his own good reasons for choosing him for economic prominence . . . in contrast to others . . . who had been singled out for poverty and drudgery.[18]

Weber is reluctant to consider the ways in which it would be possible to fulfil one's calling and to perform good works that had no bearing upon rational economic activity. He asserts that "the most important criterion" of performance in a calling "is found in private profitableness".[19] However, this appears to be his own gloss on Calvinist teaching and he provides little supporting evidence to show that the Calvinists themselves adopted such a crude and materialistic yardstick. A true believer could carry out his calling to the fullest degree and be judged in his performance on purely religious, rather than economic, criteria. Weber says as much himself. "It is true" he concedes, "that the usefulness of a calling, and thus its favour in the sight of God, is measured primarily in moral terms ..."[20] A Calvinist could feel himself to be in a state of grace, through devout conduct in his calling, even though he might be completely hopeless at making money.

The same applies to the performance of good works. The faithful were carrying out good works in so far as their behaviour was guided by the teachings of the church and inspired exclusively by the desire to serve God's purpose on earth. Good works is not to be understood in the narrow sense of 'work' or gainful activity, and its value was certainly not to be measured exclusively in the columns of the ledger.

Weber's emphasis on economic criteria and material success as the most evident proof of salvation is therefore somewhat unwarranted. The pious Calvinist would be able to detect the hand of God working in his favour in a hundred and one ways — most of them entirely unconnected with economic rationality. For example, the enjoyment of good health while others were falling sick; the survival of one's children in an age of high infant mortality; the esteem of the community bestowed upon those of exemplary asceticism; and so forth. It is clearly necessary to Weber's strong thesis that the state of the balance sheet should be regarded by the faithful as the best indication of salvation; if purely moral criteria were adopted, the energies of the Calvinist would not be so readily harnessed to capitalistic ends. All that salvation anxiety would be wasted.

IV

According to Weber, the Calvinist conception of the calling was instrumental in shaping the economic outlook of workers as well as their employers. Indeed, the spirit of capitalism could perform its alchemy on the world only if labour could be jolted out of its conventional rut. The traditional worker, Weber tells us, labours at his task only for as long as is necessary to earn his 'customary wage'. This is the basic minimum he needs to support his fixed and modest expectations. Raising his pay would not inspire greater effort, it would merely encourage him to work shorter hours, since he could earn his customary wage in less time. This is not the stuff from which rational economic activity is made.

> Wherever modern capitalism has begun its work of increasing the productivity of human labour by increasing its intensity, it has encountered the immensely stubborn resistance of this leading trait of pre-capitalistic labour.[21]

This stubborn resistance, Weber says, can only be overcome as a result of some moral or psychological transformation on the part of the worker. There must be a drastic change in the attitude to work and in the ordering of priorities between labour and leisure. Above all, the worker must purge himself of those archaic and easy-going attitudes that place more value on the use of free time than on hard graft.

Such a transformation does not come about easily or from out of the blue. It can "only be the product of a long and arduous process of education".[22] The school of instruction that first accomplished the task was Calvinism. The Calvinist conception of the calling, with its heavy accent on tireless and systematic labour for the glory of God, filled the humblest of men with an inner driving force powerful enough to snap the bonds of traditionalism. For the first time, labour was performed "as if it were an absolute end in itself, a calling".[23] With a workforce bursting with this kind of spiritual energy, the prospects for rational capitalism looked decidedly rosy. In place of a sullen and feckless labouring class, the new religious ethic offered the employer "sober, conscientious, and unusually industrious workmen, who clung to their work as to a life purpose willed by God".[24]

On this account, the Protestant ethic gives rise not only to the spirit of capitalism, but to a distinctive 'spirit of labour' as well. The logic of Weber's argument would lead us to suppose that the Calvinist worker, suffering from salvation anxiety, establishes proof of grace by exerting himself on behalf of his employer.[25] Presumably, the greater the surplus value extracted from his labour by the capitalist, the clearer the signs that he was fulfilling his calling to the proper degree.

Calvinism is thus presented as a religion that is quite exceptional in winning the hearts and minds of men, irrespective of their place in the social order. It is the one case of a religious doctrine which is exempted from Weber's general propositions concerning the selective effects of the stratification system upon organized beliefs. In his writings on the sociology of religion, Weber's standard approach is to show how the substance of belief is closely associated with the class or status position of the believers. Peasantry, proletariat, aristocracy and bourgeoisie have different material interests and life experiences, and will therefore respond to different types of religious message. In his writings on the internal stratification of religious systems, Weber could easily be mistaken for a Marxist of the old school. Indeed, Marx himself might well have considered some of Weber's statements to be a bit of a caricature of the materialist position. Here, for example, is Weber on why the peasantry is not usually susceptible to 'non-magical' beliefs:

> The lot of the peasants is so strongly tied to nature, so dependent on organic processes and natural events, and economically so little oriented to rational systematization that in general the peasantry will become a carrier of religion only when it is threatened by enslavement or proletarianization, either by domestic forces ... or by some external political power ...
>
> Only rarely does the peasantry serve as the carrier of any other sort of religion than their original magic.[26]

Because the productive life of the peasants is so much at the mercy of the elements and the uncontrollable forces of nature, they are far more likely to subscribe to magical beliefs and superstitions than to a formal religion. It would be difficult to be more materialist than that. It is the sort of thing that Engels in his dotage might have written. The same line of reasoning is used to explain the religious outlook of the feudal lords and nobility:

> As a rule, the warrior nobles, and indeed feudal powers generally, have not readily become the carriers of a rational religious ethic. The life pattern of a warrior has very little affinity with the notion of a beneficent providence, or with the systematic ethical demands of a transcendental god. Concepts like sin, salvation, and religious humility have not only seemed remote from all ruling strata, particularly the warrior nobles, but have indeed appeared reprehensible to its sense of honor.[27]

And so it goes on. Among large-scale traders and financiers, we are told, "scepticism or indifferences to religion are ... the widely diffused attitudes."[28] Small traders and artisans, on the other hand, "are disposed to accept a rational world view incorporating an ethic of compensation."[29] Bureaucrats and officials, because of the routine and orderly nature of their work activities, display "an absolute lack of feeling of a need for salvation or for any transcendental anchorage for ethics".[30]

Tell me the position that any class or stratum occupies in the division of labour or the productive process and I will tell you the general nature of the religious beliefs to which its members will subscribe. That is Weber's clear message in his sociology of religion. So carried away does he get with this tough materialist approach that he occasionally provides us with some unintended comic relief. He informs us, for example, that workers employed in indoor occupations are likely to have different religious experiences from those employed outside; "occupations which are primarily of the indoor variety in our climate, for example, in the textile trades . . . are strongly infused with sectarian or religious trends".[31] He does not go so far as to put this down to a shortage of oxygen, but it must have been a fairly close call.

In its less extravagant expressions, Weber's approach is to suggest simply that different social groups vary in their propensity to imbibe certain kinds of religious teaching. Buddhism, for example, could not generally be expected to have mass appeal to an urban proletariat. In the case of a society dominated by a single religion the same point would hold. Different social strata will tend to respond mainly to those features of doctrine that seem to resonate most closely with their own specific life-situations and experiences. Far from having a universal blanket appeal, every religion is subject to selective interpretation and endorsement by its adherents.

For some reason this does not seem to apply to Calvinism. Weber nowhere suggests that capitalists and workers put their own particular gloss upon early Protestant teachings. On the contrary, he is at some pains to show that members of both these classes accepted and acted upon moral teachings in the same way. The human representatives of capital and labour endorsed the notion of the calling with equal enthusiasm, just as if they were equal beneficiaries from the material outcome. When it comes to the analysis of Calvinism, the rough intrusions of the stratification system are mysteriously absent. We rarely if ever see this religion through the eyes of a typical labourer. The choice of Baxter as the leading exemplar of the faith thus begins to look even more suspect, given his considerable distance from the world of manual toil. The nearest Weber ever gets to acknowledging that Baxter's version of things might be closer to the outlook of the boss than of his workers is in a footnote in which he wrily remarks that in Baxter's teachings on the labour question, "the interests of God and of the employers are curiously harmonious".[32]

In claiming that the Calvinist worker internalised the notion of the calling, and thereby performed his labour as though it were an end in itself, Weber makes a further departure from his standard views. He is generally inclined to press the point that obedience and submission on the part of workers comes about in response to the threat of the 'wage whip'.[33] Slave owners and capitalists are said to be alike in the sense that both exercise coercion over their workforce, the former by physical means, the latter by money means. There is little suggestion that capitalism ever requires a normative commitment on the part of labour to operate effectively. If in a *mature* capitalist system workers still have to be dragooned into doing their jobs by the threat of the 'wage whip' it is not altogether clear why gentler methods were called for at the very birth of the system.

Weber's case is that only a moral transformation on the part of the worker could overcome the inertia of traditionalism and create a more positive attitude to labour and reward. It is worth noting that his example of the traditionalist drudge is the agricultural labourer. Give this backward soul an increase in pay and he will respond by spending less time at the plough and more at The Plough.

But, as Weber needs no telling, the spirit of capitalism was born not in the villages and pastures but in the towns and workshops. Labour had to be drawn in from the countryside to the urban centres; and, as Galbraith has recently argued, the very process of labour migration is in itself a powerfully corrosive force upon traditionalism.[34] To be uprooted from a rural community and faced with the pressing demands of urban life is a stern schooling into the ways of modernity. And the pastoral idyll of the 'customary wage' is hardly a possible option for the raw recruit to the workshop treadmill. There is, in other words, no need to conjure up the improbable notion of a joyous commitment to labour in order to account for the conduct of the early Protestant workforce. Not the slightest evidence is produced to show that a new 'spirit of labour' was abroad as a complementary partner to the spirit of capitalism. It is certainly possible that some workers really did look upon their daily grind in the sweatshop as a "life purpose willed by God". But the most telling indication that this was certainly not the common or typical attitude is provided by the capitalists' own robust methods of maintaining discipline and obedience. Marx's graphic account of the punitive regime of the Victorian capitalist workshop would suggest that employers did not bank too heavily on the voluntary compliance of their labourers to keep the production lines rolling. If Weber thought that things were very different in the workshops of the seventeenth century, he kept it to himself.

V

It should at this point be borne in mind that most of the criticisms levelled here against Weber's strong thesis do not concern the validity or otherwise of his interpretation of Calvinist doctrine. That is a matter for the theologian. Nor is it altogether necessary to contest his account of how the doctrine was actually understood and acted upon by Calvinists themselves. All the things that Weber said they believed and did could turn out to be factually true. Maybe they did suffer from salvation anxiety; maybe they did seek salvation by works; maybe they did measure success in a calling by pecuniary criteria; and so on. Even if Weber was right on all these important points, (and it is a very big if) the most intriguing question of all is still left unanswered: why did the Calvinists choose to put this particular construction on their religion and not some other construction?

Weber sets his case out in a manner to suggest that a certain set of religious precepts will inspire a predictable type of social action. Any pattern of conduct that Calvinists adopt can thus be shown to follow logically from the teachings of their ministers. Looked at in this way it can be made to seem that the faithful have little option but to behave in the manner they do. Ideas really are invested with the power to govern action.

However, as we have already seen, Weber is unusually reluctant to come to grips with the fact that any given doctrinal precept is generally capable of yielding more than one prescription for action. Now and then he seems about to confront the problem. He points out, for example, that "the doctrine of predestination could lead to fatalism if, contrary to the predominant tendencies of rational Calvinism, it were made the object of emotional contemplation."[35] The interesting question is *why* the option of emotional contemplation was rejected in favour of the alternative stance. Either course of action, once adopted, could be authenticated by the sacred texts. There was no doctrinal imperative that propelled true believers along one unavoidable path, and foreclosed all other possibilities.

The same holds true for Calvinist teachings on the problem of wealth, which Weber regards as a crucial step in the direction of rational capitalism. Baxter and the other divines gave loud and frequent warnings about the contaminating dangers of wealth and its pursuit. Weber paraphrases Baxter thus:

> Wealth as such is a great danger; its temptations never end,
> and its pursuit is not only senseless as compared with the

dominating importance of the Kingdom of God, but it is morally suspect.[36]

As Weber is aware, sentiments of this kind do not, on the face of it, seem especially congenial to the capitalist spirit. He invites us, however, to scrutinize Calvinist teachings on the subject more closely in order to uncover their 'true' meaning. A more sensitive appreciation of these teachings reveals that Calvinists did not 'really' condemn the pursuit and accumulation of wealth, despite what they actually said on this score. What they really objected to was the use of wealth for pleasurable and frivolous purposes. Wealth was not evil in itself; it only became an evil thing if used to support a life of idleness, ostentation and fleshly delights.[37]

Notwithstanding Baxter's own strictures, then, the pursuit of wealth is allegedly given the moral green light. A wink and a nod in the right direction does wonders for even the sternest doctrine. As a result of their imaginative interpretation, Calvinists were free to go in pursuit of this potentially dangerous substance, but not to lavish it upon themselves. As Weber sees it, this can lead to but one fateful conclusion:

> When the limitation of consumption is combined with this release of acquisitive activity, the inevitable practical result is obvious: accumulation of capital through ascetic compulsion to save. The restraints which were imposed upon the consumption of wealth naturally served to increase it by making possible the productive investment of capital.[38]

Modern capitalism was eased into being by the conduct of those who had nothing further from their minds. To arrive at this conclusion it is necessary to close one's eyes to the other possible uses for this unintended and unwanted wealth. Ploughing it back into the business is not the only, let alone the 'inevitable', way of offloading this malignant stuff. It could be distributed to the poor and destitute; it could be handed over to the church; it could even be used to fatten the wage packets of those whose labour had helped to create it in the first place. Reinvesting it would, of course, be the inevitable course of action for a good capitalist; but it was certainly not required of the good Calvinist. Weber cites no religious teachings that specifically urged the faithful to accumulate capital through reinvestment. The message was loud and clear only on the matter of what might *not* be done with wealth. Positive recommendations for its disposal were much less clamorous. There was sufficient ambiguity here for the successful Calvinist to decide for himself how to dispose of his wealth, other than using it for riotous living. If, as Weber says, the overwhelming response was to put it back into the business, this becomes a fact requiring explanation. To regard such conduct as completely 'natural' and unproblematic would seem to imply that the typical Calvinist was already a capitalist at heart. Indeed, Weber's entire account of Calvinist reasoning becomes highly plausible if it is understood as an answer to the question of how Franklin would have seen things if he had been a Calvinist.

VI

The corpus of religious teachings referred to by Weber under the general heading of 'Calvinism' covers a broad span of doctrine as it developed over a century or more. His ideal type of early Protestantism is, in fact, the Puritanism of the seventeenth century, as represented by Baxter and other divines. Calvin's original teachings, as Weber points out, were anything but friendly to the rational capitalist spirit. Over time, however, Calvin's successors modified and reinterpreted many of his leading ideas, in the way that the ideas of the master are usually tampered with by later generations of his acolytes. The question then arises as to why the doctrine evolved in the particular manner it did, given the other directions it could have followed from the same point of origin. Weber does not address this problem of what might be called the 'transition from Calvinism to Puritanism'.

This is not to say he was unaware of the problem. He could hardly fail to be aware of it, given his consuming interest in the relationship between beliefs and social structure. Although his principal concern had been to show the manner in which early Protestantism had brought about far-reaching changes in economic life, there was a need to redress the balance. It would thus be necessary "to investigate how Protestant Asceticism was in turn influenced in its development and its character by the totality of social conditions, especially economic."[39] What seemed to be required was a complementary study designed to demonstrate the effects of the stratification system on the peculiar evolution of early Protestantism. Had Weber managed to get round to conducting such a study he would have had to clarify and expand upon his own brand of materialism and to show how it differed from the Marxist version. Such clarification is badly needed, since despite his disdain for historical materialism there are enough hints in his work to suggest that his own final position would not have differed very much from a sophisticated Marxist one.

The sort of materialism that Weber found unpalatable was that which viewed Calvinism and the Reformation in general as a direct product of class struggle and economic change. This was the view that the emergent bourgeoisie in some sense created a new religious outlook that corresponded to their material interests. Looked at from this angle, the new class was responsible for ushering in both Calvinism and capitalism; the religious precepts embodied in the former served as a convenient moral covering for the exploitative practices inherent in the latter.

Weber was naturally well aware of the close alliance between Calvinism and the rising bourgeoisie. He speaks of this class as being the main 'bearers' of the Protestant ethic, rather in the way that Marx speaks of it as being the main bearers of new productive forces.[40] However, to identify a certain class or stratum as the bearer of a certain religious ethic is not to claim that the class in question itself created this ethic. As Weber sees it, religious ideas are not spawned by class interests or similar material forces. A system of ethics can originate and evolve in response to purely doctrinal exigencies. Heresies and schisms generally occur as a result of learned disputations among the sacerdotal elite, not as a result of murmuring by the masses. New meanings are read into old texts more easily by those who inhabit the elevated world of ideas. The connection between their mental productions and the grubby preoccupations of mundane life is generally rather slender.

Weber would further say, however, that the production of ideas is not to be confused with their distribution. Although spiritual virtuosos may reveal the word of God in new and dramatic ways, there is no guarantee that their message will be heeded. Many messiahs appear only to sink without trace; others capture the souls of multitudes. It is when we seek to account for the absorption or rejection of beliefs that social and material factors may properly be brought into play. Thus, while Weber would consider it absurd to explain the Reformation as an outcome of class struggle, he would not consider it absurd to suggest that competing religious systems arising out of the Reformation varied systematically in their appeal to different social strata. His general view would seem to lend itself to a Darwinian analogy. That is, new belief systems may spring up with the unpredictability of genetic mutations, but their survival and growth will depend upon the favourableness of the environment. Looked at from the other end of the process, individuals or groups 'select' the complex of ideas that seems to answer most closely to their existential needs. The social circumstances of a given class or status group could be said to promote only *structure and agency*

a general disposition to a certain kind of religious (or secular) ethic; the circumstances do not in any sense create that ethic. It is indeed possible that a general disposition could go unsatisfied; or, conversely, that an 'available' set of beliefs could find no takers on any real scale. There is thus an important element of contingency in the relationship between ideas and social structure.

Weber's understanding of this relationship, as reconstructed above, does seem rather more compelling than the materialist view upon which he poured his scorn. It would be difficult for it not to be, given that the materialist view in question was of such a Neanderthal kind. But there is a more refined version of materialism, less extant in his day than it is in ours, which is virtually indistinguishable from his own. The refined version concedes that religious ideas, like other cultural artefacts, are able to enjoy a considerable amount of 'relative autonomy' from the imperious demands of the material infrastructure. In the rarified atmosphere of the ideological realm, spiritual life can unfold according to laws that are not under the direct jurisdiction of political economy. However, once they are in play, religious and moral ideas can be, and generally are, drawn into service as legitimating agencies. From this perspective, the bourgeoisie would be said not to have manufactured the Protestant ethic, but to have seized upon that ethic as a means of acquiring moral endorsement for its secular activities. The success and spread of Calvinism could then be attributed to the presence of a new, ascendant class whose members could bathe in the assurance of super-natural support for doing what came naturally.

This way of looking at the matter is obviously a good deal closer to Weber's own. To put himself at any distance from it, he would have needed to argue quite vigorously against the claim that Calvinism's main contribution was to provide moral covering for a class that was already imbued with the capitalist spirit. If the spirit of capitalism was independently abroad, 'carried' in the practices of a rising class, the case for Calvinism as the very precursor of this spirit would be badly dented. To say that the Protestant ethic served merely to legitimate the capitalist spirit is obviously very different from saying that it produced it.

If in his unwritten complementary essay Weber had attempted to rebut the refined materialist view, he would have run into some difficulty. This is because he himself frequently makes the point that any social group which hankers after a privileged place in the sun will always try to justify its actions by moral arguments. One of the recurring themes in his writings on domination is that the powerful, and all contenders for power, invariably attempt to convince themselves and others of the ethical propriety of their claims. Even despots need to believe in their own political legitimacy. Moreover, Weber often regards religion as an instrument that is well suited to this purpose. Indeed, he sometimes goes so far as to say that, for some groups at least, this is the only or principal purpose of religion. In one of those stark formulations that are the hallmark of his sociology of religion, he declares that

> Other things being equal, strata with high social and economic privilege ... assign to religion the primary function of *legitimizing* their own life pattern and situation in the world ... What the privileged classes require of religion, if anything at all, is this legitimation.[41]

The sophisticated materialist could hardly have expressed it more forcefully. Like the materialist, too, Weber sometimes sees religion as a weapon of ideological control and pacification. According to him, bureaucratic classes in Europe, although themselves fairly irreligious, have been "compelled to pay more official respect to the religiosity of the churches in the interest of mass domestication".[42]

Given his own emphatic claims about the legitimizing functions of religion, Weber is not too well placed to deny such a role to early Protestantism. The proposition that Calvinism and its offshoots provided a convenient moral cloak for the materialistic drives of a rising bourgeoisie has a distinctly Weberian ring to it. There are good indications to suggest, in fact, that Weber would not wish to disavow such a proposition. During a visit to the United States in 1904 he witnessed a baptism ceremony that seems to have made a deep impression on him. As one of the novices underwent total immersion, the following exchange took place between Weber and a companion. The companion speaks first:

> "Look at him" he said. "I told you so!"
> When I asked him after the ceremony "Why did you anticipate the baptism of that man?" he answered
> "Because he wants to open a bank in M."
> "Are there so many Baptists around that he can make a living?"
> "Not at all, but once being baptised he will get the patronage of the whole region and he will outcompete everybody."[43]

Here, then, is a case of a young man who needs no introduction to the capitalist spirit, but who does need the ethical imprimatur that membership in a Protestant sect can bestow. As Weber puts it, "sect membership meant a certificate of moral qualification and especially of business morals for the individual."[44] It is significant that Weber does not appear to regard this incident, and the conclusion to be drawn from it, as in any way exceptional. Although it occurred at a time and place far removed from the original setting of early Protestantism, there is never any suggestion that the motives and conduct of the young Baptist were different from those of his seventeenth century Puritan equivalents. Rather the opposite;

> the modern functions of American sects and sectlike associations . . . are revealed as straight derivatives, rudiments, and survivals of those conditions which once prevailed in all asceticist sects and conventicles.[45]

The ceremony that he witnessed in early twentieth century America might thus have been different only in its ritual forms from similar ceremonies in seventeenth century Europe. The implication is that those who were already and independently imbued with the spirit of capitalism could also have decided that membership of Baxter's flock would be a seal of commercial approval. How nice for them to know, too, that in turning a quick penny they were following the path of righteousness. If Weber ever demurred from the view that early Protestant religion served as a legitimating device for the principle 'bearers' of the capitalist spirit he did not make his objection plain.[46] Yet, in the light of his strong thesis, some such objection — or at least some clarification of his position — was certainly called for.

In the unwritten essay on the effects of social structure on religious beliefs, we can charitably assume that Weber would have clarified his views on the troublesome issue of causation versus legitimation by seeking to assign a different *weighting* to each. It is unlikely that he would have had much truck with the vacuous proposition that these things simply interacted upon one another in a fully reciprocal fashion. Weber was always intent upon identifying the prime movers in social action; since only a half-wit would wish to deny that the complex patterns of social life are the product of many different factors and forces, the task is to allocate causal priorities to these various elements. The most unimaginative, and most improbable, account would be one that proposed that all the social factors involved contributed in equal degree to the final outcome. To say that the Protestant ethic was, in equal measure, both the originator of the capitalist spirit and its legitimating cover, would be a conclusion that would set Weber's teeth on edge.

In addressing himself to these numerous matters, it is very likely that Weber would have taken it upon himself to explore the more general problem of the 'transition from Calvinism to Puritanism.' Given his standard line of approach in the sociology of religion, we may safely assume that he would have sought to point up the association between early Protestant teachings and the stratification system. In particular, he might have tried to show the extent to which the peculiar evolution of Protestant ideas was related to contemporary disturbances in the class structure. Looked at in that way, early Protestantism would have to be treated as a doctrine capable of providing several alternative recipes for social action. As Weber recognized, "it is not the ethical *doctrine* of a religion, but that form of ethical conduct upon which *premiums* are placed that matters".[47] This being so, it would be necessary to explain why certain forms of ethical conduct were selected out for 'premium' treatment while others were not. Someone of Weber's cast of mind would naturally look in the direction of class and status group interests for possible leads. He would then have had to redirect his attention from the sayings of Baxter to the doings of a proto-typical Calvinist capitalist – the strangely absent figure in his analysis. Seen in the light of early capitalists' needs and preferences, the kinds of ethical teachings singled out for emphasis might have struck Weber as being fairly predictable. In addition, when inspecting the problem from the other end of the stratification system, it is more than likely that he would have had second thoughts about the inspirational effects of Calvinism upon the emergent working class, as compared with the effect of the 'wage whip'.

In order to assess the influence of social structure upon the evolution of Calvinist beliefs and practices, Weber would have had to give his investigation a comparative slant. He would have needed to show whether or not the transition from Calvinism to Puritanism was paralleled by the evolution of contemporary Catholic doctrine. Weber generally takes medieval Catholicism as an ideal-typical traditional religion and then contrasts this version with the Puritanism of the seventeenth century. The possibility that the 'premiums' placed upon the ethical conduct of Catholics also underwent selective change and emphasis in the post-medieval period is never seriously considered. Clearly, any discovery that interpretative tendencies friendly to the capitalist spirit had arisen within Catholicism also, would have important repercussions on Weber's strong and weak theses. As far as the strong thesis is concerned, it would raise fresh doubts about the claim that the origins of the new spirit were to be found in an exclusively Protestant ethic. As far as the weak thesis is concerned, it would undermine the claim that early Protestantism enjoyed a unique affinity with the spirit of capitalism. This claim in any case raises a cluster of other problems about Weber's general procedure. These concern, in particular his ideal-type constructs of the world religions and his use of the comparative method.

VII

The real significance of Calvinism, according to the weak thesis, is that it did not in the least hamper the development of a rational economic mentality. Weber presents the other great world religions as direct impediments to the efflorescence of the capitalist spirit. Medieval Catholicism, Hinduism, Buddhism, Confucianism, Islam and the rest, were saturated with magical beliefs and superstitions that were thoroughly at variance with any kind of rational outlook or systematic worldly conduct. Weber's remarks on Hinduism would serve quite well as a capsule statement of his general view of the world religions.

> The core of the obstacle did not lie in ... particular difficulties, which every one of the great religious systems in its way has placed, or has seemed to place, in the way of the modern economy. The core of the obstruction was rather embedded in the 'spirit' of the whole system.[48]

Weber's studies of the world religions could be seen, to a large extent, as a comparative exercise designed to throw into high relief the singularity of Calvinism. This was the religion that had divested itself most thoroughly of magic and superstition; it forced the believer to turn away from the irrational practice of seeking solace through sacraments, images and priestly intervention, and to confront the world alone in the sight of God. All other religions, in their various ways, encouraged man's adaptation to the world. Calvinism alone drove him to transform it. Here at last was a religion that would not smother at birth the delicate spirit of economic rationality. It is as though the capitalist spirit could arise, potentially, from many different sources and in many different places, but that its typical fate was to run foul of hostile religious forces. In pockets of northern Europe, in the sixteenth and seventeenth centuries, these hostile forces were exceptionally absent.

In his characterization of the world religions, Weber sets up a series of ideal-types. Only the most salient features of any belief system are incorporated into the general construct. This necessarily entails the accentuation of some features and the exclusion or devaluation of others. In the case of Calvinism, it is noticeable that Weber heavily underscores those teachings that could be said to be broadly compatible with the capitalist ethos, while discounting those elements that appear to jar with it. When it comes to the other major religions, the opposite procedure is adopted. Elements in Hinduism, Confucianism, Judaism, and the rest, that seem to square quite well with economic rationality are accorded only a peripheral place in the model, while those elements that are at variance with such an outlook are given a central place. As a number of other authorities on these religions have noted, it is perfectly possible to construct ideal-types in which Weber's priorities are reversed. Singer, for example, has suggested that Hinduism contained many doctrinal teachings that were potentially 'available for the support of rational economic action.[49] Rodinson and Turner have each made similar points about Islam.[50] It is, thus, at least debateable whether the 'core of the obstruction' is really an intrinsic quality of these religions, or whether it is the product of Weber's ideal types. Moreover, his typification of Calvinism has been declared by some authorities to be a badly distorted one. Sombart, for example, argued that the teachings of the Puritan divines, including Baxter, were weighted predominantly against anything smacking of a capitalist spirit.[51]

The question here is not so much whose construct is right and whose is wrong. Rather, it is whether it is ever really possible to set up an ideal-type that is uncontaminated by the explanatory use to which it is being put. As we have earlier seen, Weber was fully aware that constructs of this kind were bound to be morally loaded, and that by changing the criteria for the selection of core features, the final construct could be altered accordingly. Any ideal-type, therefore, is necessarily built around a scaffolding of presuppositions which the investigator brings to the enquiry from the outset. It is highly improbable to suppose that Weber embarked upon his studies of the world religions in a spirit of complete intellectual agnosticism. The typifications that emerge from these studies are hardly the product of open-minded curiosity. This is just as well, perhaps, since those who submerge themselves in a morass of data without a powerful set of working hunches are unlikely ever to rise to the surface.

This being said, it does not dispose of the problem of how we are to decide between equally plausible but conflicting ideal-types. The master himself offered no guidance on how to evaluate the competing claims of his own ideal-type of Calvinism and Sombart's version. This is of no small importance, since if we accept Sombart's version, even the weak thesis is badly damaged. Calvinism would be shown to have no special affinity with the capitalist spirit. Similarly, of course, if we were persuaded by those constructs of eastern religions in which the 'core of the obstruction' had been removed, then Calvinism would again cease to be quite so unusual in its tolerance of the capitalist spirit. There is no need to complicate matters even more by considering the other half of the equation – the spirit of capitalism. Suffice it to say that if we were to accept Marx's typification of this spirit, instead of Weber's, any special affinity with the Protestant ethic would be even more difficult to detect.

VIII

One of the reasons why Weber went to such unusual lengths to try and show the failure of the capitalist spirit to develop properly in the Orient was to demonstrate that in the absence of a motivational drive even the most promising institutional conditions would not be employed for rational economic ends. Capitalism of the modern variety could only make headway if both substance and spirit – the structural and normative supports – were present. In his comparative studies, Weber underlines the point that in places like India and China the substance was present in sufficient degree to give capitalism a fighting chance.

> For centuries urban development in India paralleled that of the Occident at many points. The contemporary rational number system, the technical basis of all 'calculability', is of Indian origin ... Arithmetic and algebra are considered to have been independently developed in India ... the Indians cultivated rational science (including mathematics and grammar) ... Indian justice developed numerous forms which could have served capitalistic purposes as easily and well as corresponding institutions in our own medieval law. The autonomy of the merchant stratum in law-making was at least equivalent to that of our own medieval merchants. Indian handicrafts and occupational specialization were highly developed. From the standpoint of possible capitalistic development, the acquisitiveness of Indians of all strata left little to be desired, and nowhere is to be found ... such high evaluation of wealth. Yet modern capitalism did not develop indigenously before or during the English rule.[52]

Similarly, Chinese and other non-western civilizations do not seem to have been riddled with structural impediments to the indigenous development of rational capitalism.

It is obviously not a question of deeming the Chinese 'naturally ungifted' for the demands of capitalism. But compared to the Occident, the varied conditions which externally favoured the origin of capitalism in China did not suffice to create it. Likewise capitalism did not originate in occidental or oriental Antiquity, or in India, or where Islam held sway. Yet in each of these areas different and favourable circumstances seemed to facilitate its rise.[53]

Weber did not, of course, suggest that everything on the institutional side was favourable to the emergence of capitalism in the Orient. Some things were not. But the overall balance between positive and negative conditions was weighted towards the positive side. This was precisely similar to the situation in the west. Weber reminds us that there were various structural impediments to the rise of capitalism in Europe too – impediments, moreover, which some Oriental societies were not afflicted by. For example,

Circumstances which are usually considered to have been obstacles to capitalist development in the Occident had not existed for thousands of years in China. Such circumstances as the fetters of feudalism, landlordism and, in part also, the guild system were lacking there. Besides, a considerable part of the various trade-restricting monopolies which were characteristic of the Occident did not apparently exist in China.[54]

Weber thus underscores the point that east and west could not be said to have differed profoundly in their preparedness for capitalism. Each in their different way had sufficiently strong institutional and material foundations to support rational economic action on the grand scale. The fact that the new system arose exclusively in the west must therefore be explained by the additive effect of something that was present in the west alone. This extra something was the spirit of capitalism. And the reason it was missing everywhere else was because none of these other places had a set of beliefs equivalent to the Protestant ethic.

Parsons, among others, regards Weber's procedure here as an exemplary use of the comparative method.[55] By holding structural factors constant, it was possible to test the independent effect of the religious variable. Naturally, the validity of this procedure depends very much upon the claim that structural factors can be treated as constants. And it is on this crucial point that Weber is at his most maddeningly inconsistent.

In some parts of his work, as we have just seen, he presses the case that eastern civilizations possessed as many social and institutional supports for capitalism as were found in the west. In other parts of his work he sets about demolishing this case with a vengeance. Many sections of *Economy and Society* and his *General Economic History* are devoted to drawing the sharpest possible contrast between the institutional arrangements of Occident and Orient. We are told that the city, for example, developed along entirely different lines in east and west.[56] In the east, the city was almost always under the dominion of the central powers or the military and was never able to win the legal and political autonomy enjoyed by cities in late medieval Europe. Consequently, there was no opportunity for the rise of an independent burgher class in the east. With regard to property rights, urban land in the west was always treated as an alienable commodity; this was rarely if ever the case in the Orient. Similarly with regard to civic rights and formal individual liberties:

> the contrast between the East and the ancient world on the one hand and the medieval West on the other with respect to the legal status of the person was absolute.[57]

In the west, law and justice were administered according to rational procedures and impersonal rules; in the east, the administration of justice was highly 'irrational', in that it was dispensed along arbitrary lines according to the whims and idiosyncracies of the high and mighty. This was the 'Kadi-justice' of Sultans, Nawabs, Caliphs, and the like.

Most important of all, perhaps, was the fact that Europe alone could boast of deeply-rooted laws and institutions that guaranteed and enforced the rights of contract and exchange. Weber says that in order for a rational economic order to flourish it is absolutely necessary that there should be

> an unambiguous and clear legal system, that would be free of irrational administrative arbitrariness ... that would also offer firm guaranties of the legally binding character of contracts ... [58]

No oriental society got anywhere near to establishing these indispensable safeguards for contractual relations. And so the catalogue continues. Virtually every institution that falls under Weber's scrutiny is shown to have an entirely different form and function in the east compared with the west. This applies not just to political and legal arrangements but to culture also. Weber regards the music, painting, and architecture of the west to be wholly unlike the music, painting and architecture of the Orient on the grounds that the former are based on uniquely 'rational' principles.[59] Weber's extremely liberal use of the code word 'rational' to describe all things western is on a par with his fondness for the word 'magical' when describing the religions of the east. Although he does not use the term 'Asiatic despotism' to refer to societies viewed through ethnocentric western eyes, he might just as well have done.

If, on Weber's own reckoning, the urban structure, property relations, the legal and administrative system, the political functions of the state, and very much else besides, were completely different as between east and west, it is obviously not possible to test for the separate effect of the religious variable. Structural factors are anything but constants. Weber regards the whole complex of linked institutions that arose in the west to be essential preconditions for the rise of capitalism. This was the necessary 'substance' of capitalism. Since this substance was apparently missing in India, China and other non-western civilizations, the fact that the capitalist spirit was also missing would have little explanatory importance. Even had this spirit made its appearance, via religion or from some other source, it would have had precious little matter upon which to work its chemistry. The only safe conclusion that emerges from all this is that the retardation of capitalism in the Orient was due to a combination of normative and structural impediments. Maybe some of the tortured convolutions of Weber's argument could be put down to an understandable reluctance to accept that such a mountain of labour could produce such a mouse of a conclusion.

The converse proposition would also seem to hold; namely, that capitalism arose in the west because of the fortuitous combination of spirit and substance. However, in the western context this proposition is not quite so commonplace. This is because capitalism originated not in Europe as a whole, but only in particular regions. Europe is thus a more suitable laboratory in which to test the proposition. In Weber's account, the institutional or substantive preconditions for rational capitalism were established throughout most of Europe. The spirit of capitalism, on the other hand, originated only in those places where ascetic Protestantism was a vital force. In other words, structural conditions *could* in this case be held constant, and religion treated as a variable. The independent effect of the religious ethic could thus be properly assessed. Wherever Calvinism sank deep roots in Europe we should expect to find rational capitalism making its appearance. The failure of capitalism to emerge under such favourable circumstances would indicate that something was badly wrong with the theory. The Scottish case seems to offer one such indication.

Ascetic Protestantism was well established in Scotland by the end of the sixteenth century. By the end of the seventeenth century the brand of reformed Calvinism taught by the Scots equivalents of Baxter was entrenched to a degree that was virtually unrivalled in Europe. Yet, as all authorities agree, capitalism failed to develop independently in Scotland. When it did appear, late in the day, it was largely as an English import.

In a recent and highly commendable attempt to salvage Weber's theory, Marshall has argued that the poor showing of capitalism north of the border, despite the abundance of Protestant energy, was due to the lack of supporting structural conditions.[60] The spirit was present without the substance. Among the various inhibiting factors he mentions are the medieval structure of trade, the ravages of war, social upheavals over religion, protectionist commercial policies, the smallness of local markets, and backward agricultural methods.[61] He concludes that

> Scots capitalists did not lack appropriate motivation to 'capitalist accumulation' but their designs were, for more than a century, frustrated by the backwardness of the economic structure of the country, in other words, by the conditions of action that circumscribed their activities. Under these circumstances, the modern capitalist economy was relatively slow to develop in Scotland, but this is precisely what Weber himself would have predicted.[62]

If Weber is to be vindicated in this way, we need to be convinced that the structural supports for capitalism were exceptionally weak in Scotland. But it is doubtful whether conditions north of the border were really so different from those in the south. Wars and social upheavals over religion were certainly no strangers to England in the seventeenth century. Old fashioned ways of agriculture and the trading restrictions imposed by mercantilist policies were by no means unique to Scotland. Moreover, it was precisely these 'traditionalist' and backward methods of doing things that the capitalist spirit was supposed to be able to transform. The traditionalist mentality itself cannot be cited as an inhibiting factor since this was everywhere the pre-capitalist norm.

Remember, too, that Weber did not say that everything on the structural front had to be just right before capitalism could seize its chance. All that was necessary was that the balance between favourable and unfavourable factors should be tilted in the direction of the former. And on that score, Scotland comes out remarkably well. It possessed all the really important institutional supports for capitalism that

Weber himself enumerated. Scotland could boast a thoroughly rational system of law and administration. Its towns were fiercely independent of control by the central powers. Property rights, contract and exchange relations were fully guaranteed and enforced by law. The civic status of the individual was also given formal recognition. In these and other ways Scotland could lay claim to being an ideal-typical rational state, as defined by Weber. With this formidable array of advantages, together with a rampant Calvinism, capitalism could hardly have wished for a better start. Its refusal to put in its expected appearance is not the best advertisement for Weber's thesis.

3
Domination and Legitimacy

> Domination in the most general sense is one of the most
> important elements of social action. Of course, not every form
> of social action reveals a structure of dominancy. But in most
> of the varieties of social action domination plays a consider-
> able role, even where it is not obvious at first sight ... Without
> exception every sphere of social action is profoundly influenced
> by structures of dominancy.[1]

This is the leitmotif that runs through all Weber's political sociology.
Societies and their lesser parts are held together not so much through
contractual relations or moral consensus as through the exercise of
power. Where harmony and order apparently prevail, the threatened
use of force is never altogether absent. Inside the velvet glove is always
an iron fist. The terminology of violence, coercion and force is as
natural to Weber's sociology as the terminology of moral integration
is to Durkheim's.

In his discussion of the nature of the state, for example, Weber
adopted a stance that was some considerable distance away from the
prevailing idea. The doctors of philosophy in his time and place looked
upon the state as an object of reverence, one of the best and noblest
of man's creations. The state was an almost mystical entity that inhabited

the rarified atmosphere above society, untouched by the squalid bickering of parties, classes and interest groups. This metaphysical view of the state was to some extent bound up with contemporary movements of national unification and the drawing and consolidation of territorial boundaries. It served as an attractive doctrine in the struggle against enemies within and without the gates. Loyalty to the state, and to the very idea of the state, could be held as the ultimate political commitment, transcending loyalty to all local particularisms and private interests.

Seen against this background of quasi-religious adulation, Weber's conception of the state was downright heretical. In his view, the most notable feature of the state was the fact that it could successfully lay claim to a monopoly of the legitimate use of violence. He held that "violent social action is obviously something absolutely primordial."[2] Every social group, of whatever kind, is prepared to resort to violence in the protection of its interests. The state is different only in the sense that it claims the sole right to use force upon anyone and everyone living within its territorial jurisdiction.

In Weber's writings, the concept of the state is clearly differentiated from that of nation. The nation was a cultural community that was held together by the powerful bonds of language and the moral sentiments transmitted by the mother tongue. Weber's idea of the nation was in fact very much akin to that abstraction known to Durkheim as 'society'. Although nation and state were two quite separate things they did require one another for mutual survival. Nations needed to become states in order to defend the boundaries of the cultural community against erosion or assault by predatory neighbours. States needed to become nations in order to lay the foundations of internal unity.

Weber's emphasis upon the territorial component of the state is one of the features that sets off his position from that of Marx and his followers. Marx too, of course, portrayed the state as anything but a benign and tender instrument of rule. And Lenin's terse definition of the state as 'bodies of armed men' left little room for ambiguity about its violent qualities. In Marxist theory, however, the state is understood mainly as an agency of internal social control; the violence it contains is unleashed by one class upon another as part of the general process of exploitation. Those who would transform society must seize the state from within in order to impose and maintain their own class domination. There is relatively small concern with the uses of state power to protect the boundaries of the nation against external enemies. In any case, the idea of territorial defence would not really have much place in a doctrine that taught that the proletariat had no homeland.

For Weber, the passionate nationalist, the territorial question was paramount. He says comparatively little about the role of the state in relation to class structure and exploitation. The security of Germany's eastern borders and the country's precarious place in international affairs was much more on his mind. Weber believed that every powerful political community had a natural urge to expand and to increase its sway over others. This was due in large measure to the fact that rulers and military leaders could best enhance their prestige and prosecute their own careers by the aggressive expansion of state territory.

> Power for their political community means power for themselves, as well as the prestige based on this power. For the bureaucrat and the officer, an expansion of power means more office positions, more sinecures, and better opportunities for promotion.[3]

Because of this socially determined impulse to enlarge their territory, political communities were always a potential threat to their neighbours. In such an unfriendly world any idea that the state could wither away was utterly laughable. Weber was so insistent upon characterising the modern state as an instrument of violence that he was prepared to deny that states can usefully be classified according to the aims and policies they pursue.

> Sociologically, the state cannot be defined in terms of its ends ... Ultimately, one can define the modern state sociologically only in terms of the specific *means* peculiar to it ... namely, the use of physical force.[4]

What this imples, of course, is that no really helpful distinction can be drawn between different types of state — capitalist, socialist, fascist, bourgeois, military, totalitarian, or whatever. Since they all employ roughly the same physical means of violence, differences in political design and purpose are somewhat secondary. Dictatorship and democracy, strawberry and vanilla.

The question that Weber does not feel has to be asked is whether different forms of state might vary systematically in the degree of violence that they use. Nor does he raise the matter, so important to Marxist theory, of whether the state is selective in its use of force, coming down more heavily on some sections of the community than others. One is left wondering what all this violence is supposed to be used *for*. There is, again, little attempt by Weber to construe things from the actors' point of view. Those who live beneath the shadow of the state generally have quite firm ideas and feelings of their own about the behaviour of their political masters. Weber's lofty assurance that one state is pretty much like another would not necessarily cut much ice among those on the receiving end of some ancient or modern tyranny.

II

These and other related matters are raised anew in Weber's general treatise on domination. Domination is held to be a special case of power. It is a more refined and restricted concept than power in that not all uses of power would qualify as domination. There are, to begin with, two quite contrasting and opposed types of domination. One arises from monopolistic control of economic resources in the market-place; the other rests upon the authority of office. Domination in the marketplace is exercised indirectly, through the mediation of commodities and resources. Those who suffer domination in this way are formally free to act in accordance with their rational economic interests. Domination on the basis of authority, on the other hand, is exercised directly over those who have a 'duty' to obey. Whereas no-one is expected to obey the capitalist or the banker out of a sense of duty, everyone is expected to obey the patriarch or the prince precisely on these grounds: rational self-interest does not come into it.[5]

Weber is concerned only with this second type of domination. That is to say, "in our terminology *domination* shall be identical with *authoritarian power of command*", to the exclusion of that kind of domination wielded by the hidden hand of the market.[6] Moreover, it is not enough simply for commands to be issued; they must also be obeyed before we can speak of true domination. For sociological purposes, commands that are ignored must be treated as something other than domination. In other words, obedience or compliance is built into the very definition of domination.

It is important to note that Weber defines domination not merely as a structure of command that elicits obedience, but as obedience that is willingly given. Domination means that commands are complied with "as if the ruled had made the content of the command the maxim of their conduct for its very own sake."[7] In case there should be any lingering doubt on this point, Weber makes it crystal clear that a positive commitment on the part of the subordinate to the authority they obey is a cardinal feature of domination.

The merely external fact of the order being obeyed is not
sufficient to signify domination in our sense; we cannot over-
look the meaning of the fact that the command is accepted as
a 'valid' norm.[8]

To obey out of a sense of fear or through sheer expediency would not
suffice; normative endorsement is absolutely crucial. Domination, for
Weber, is thus another way of speaking of 'legitimate authority'.

The upshot of all this is that structures of authority which rely
more upon coercion than upon willing compliance are excluded from
Weber's typology of domination. This is more than a little surprising in
view of his repeated stress upon the ubiquity of force and violence in
human affairs. If the analysis of domination is to be confined to those
systems of authoritative command in which the underdogs readily
conspire in their own submission, the scope of the enquiry is bound to
be somewhat limited. Weber was more aware than most that the history
of political systems was not exactly a chronicle of the affections
displayed by the lowly towards their masters. His assumption seems to
have been that regimes cannot exist by coercion alone, and that some
degree of moral support from below is necessary to the long term
survival of any authority system. He does in fact say that the "con-
tinued exercise of every domination . . ." always entails some successful
claim to legitimacy.[9] Regimes that fail to establish such claims are
presumably destined for the rubbish-tip of history.

It can readily be conceded that all authority structures rely upon a
variety of means, including the means of legitimation, to keep themselves intact. In the typical case, a combination of physical coercion,
moral persuasion, and material inducements would be employed in
various degrees. Weber certainly recognized that more was required
than an elaborate exercise in moral rearmament; the carrot and the
stick would also find ample employment. What he might reasonably
have been expected to do, then, was to classify authority systems
according to their different combination or mix of these different
elements of social control. That is to say, regimes could have been
classified on the basis of whether the predominant means of control
were coercive, normative or instrumental. A proper distinction could
then have been made between authority systems that relied mainly on
the use or threat of force and those that relied mainly on the powers of
moral persuasion. On this arrangement, only systems that approximated
to the latter model would qualify as examples of 'legitimate authority'.
Legitimate authority could thus be treated as a matter of degree and
not an all or nothing affair. All systems might strive to attain it, but not

all succeed in equal measure. Some still have to fall back on the use of rougher measures more than they would ideally like.

Weber's reluctance to regard legitimate authority as a commodity that could vary considerably between different systems is very much in line with his refusal to classify states according to their political ends and practices. It could well be that in defining domination as legitimate authority he simply took it as understood that normative means were only to be regarded as the predominant, not the exclusive, technique of social control. Even so, this would still not overcome the objection that regimes and authority structures more noted for their brutality than for their ability to inspire affection are allowed no place in the typology of domination. Since the balance between normative control and physical coercion is probably tipped towards the latter in most authority systems past and present, the effect is to reduce drastically the general applicability of his schema.

There is a further problem that Weber does not fully consider. This concerns the manner in which normative compliance and legitimacy is actually brought about. A subordinate group or class could accept commands as 'valid norms' out of a genuine belief in the worthiness of those in control and support for the aims they were pursuing. This kind of popular support for a regime is sometimes found during the heady, optimistic period immediately following a revolution. Normative compliance is spontaneous rather than engineered. Alternatively, such compliance may be brought about as a consequence of total powerlessness. Oppressed social groups sometimes absorb ideas about the superiority of their masters as a form of adaptation to their plight. Under certain circumstances coercive powers can thus be employed in such a way as to bend fractious hearts and minds towards allegiance. Weber makes no distinction between normative compliance that springs from voluntary commitment and that which is grounded in a long term strategy for survival. The questions raised by Marx and his followers concerning the relationship between coercion and compliance are closed off by Weber's approach to the matter. This approach has no place for notions like 'hegemony'. If subordinate groups accept the commands of their masters as valid norms, the domination of the masters is legitimate, and that is the end of it. How and why this process comes about is not thought worth considering.

Weber was of course fully alive to the fact that obedience to commands could occur for reasons other than moral respect for the people in control or from a sense of loyalty to the system.

Loyalty may be hypocritically simulated by individuals or by whole groups on purely opportunistic grounds, or carried out in practice for reasons of material self-interest. Or people may submit from individual weakness and helplessness because there is no acceptable alternative.[10]

He immediately goes on to say, however, that "these considerations are not decisive for the classification of types of domination. What is important is the fact that in a given case the particular claim to legitimacy is to a significant degree ... treated as 'valid'.[11] Forms or types of domination differ only by dint of the kinds of claims put out by those in command concerning the legitimacy of their own rule.

These claims to legitimacy are of three broad types: *traditional, charismatic* and *legal-rational.* Weber refers to these as the "three inner justifications" or "basic legitimations of domination".[12] *Traditional domination* rests upon the appeal to the sanctity of custom and immemorial tradition. This is the type of domination exercised by patriarchs, tribal elders and the like. *Charismatic domination* rests upon the personal magnetism of an heroic figure, someone who possesses the gift of grace. Prophets, saints, and revolutionary leaders are the standard examples. *Legal-rational domination* rests on the appeal to the propriety of formally enacted rules and statutes. Bureaucracy is the archetypal case of this type of domination. Weber's three types of domination are thus three different grounds on which the demands for obedience are based.

Type of domination	*Grounds for claiming obedience*
Traditional	Obey me because this is what our people have always done.
Charismatic	Obey me because I can transform your life.
Legal-rational	Obey me because I am your lawfully appointed superior.

All people in authority, Weber says, concoct myths about their own superiority and natural fitness to rule. These myths or inner justifications are necessary for their self-assurance and their sense of political propriety. Legitimations are the moral vocabularies of those who speak with the voice of authority. There is, though, an important difference between legitimations and legitimacy. Legitimations are the claims that dominant groups make about themselves — claims that they would naturally wish everyone else to accept. Legitimacy, on the other hand, refers to the condition in which such claims have in fact been accepted and endorsed by subordinate groups. That is, the grounds upon which obedience is claimed are accepted as valid by those who are expected to do the obeying. Legitimations emanate from on high, but legitimacy is bestowed from below.

Weber could have proposed his three types of legitimation while keeping an open mind on the question of whether or not they were accepted by the people to whom they were addressed. Had he been seized by the comparative urge he might have asked whether the legitimations put out by traditional, charismatic, and legal-rational authorities differed in the degree to which they were actually endorsed by the masses. Are the claims of charismatic leaders more readily accepted than the claims of bureaucratic officials? Do different strata of the population differ in their susceptibility to the three different legitimating myths? Instead of asking questions of this kind, Weber proceeds as though widespread endorsement of all three types of legitimation was typically found among all and sundry. The three different types of 'dominant legitimations' have metamorphosed into three different types of 'legitimate domination'. It is as if Weber simply assumed the correctness of Marx's dictum that the prevailing ideas in any society are the ideas of its ruling class. Since the powerful are always in a position to inject their own conceptions into the life-stream of society, the attainment of legitimacy never poses much of a problem.

Had Weber treated the conferment of legitimacy as a rather more uncertain and precarious business he could have broadened the scope of his analysis in several ways. He could, for example, have considered the not infrequent cases in which the dominant class *fails* to establish its moral credentials in the eyes of the people; or cases in which legitimacy is initially granted but subsequently withdrawn. In other words he could have given conceptual recognition to that condition now diagnosed as 'legitimation crisis'. Maybe he would have done so if he had had the opportunity to experience a little more of Weimar. All that he says on this score is that legitimacy is most readily bestowed upon regimes in which the class and status orders are relatively stable and undisturbed, but that legitimacy may be withdrawn when exploitation has become "unambiguously and openly visible to everyone".[13] He does not, however, tell us what type of domination would then prevail, when the commands of the powerful were no longer accepted as morally valid. In Weber's schema there is no such category as *illegitimate* domination, even though he clearly recognizes it as an empirical probability.

Had he redirected his attention from the advertisements of legitimation to the granting of legitimacy he would have been forced to shift his focus from the perceptions of elites to the perceptions of the masses. In so doing he would have found it necessary to supplement his sociology of command with a sociology of compliance. At times it does appear as though he is about to embark upon such an enterprise. In his lecture on *Politics as a Vocation* he is prompted to ask the leading question, "When and why do men obey?"[14] And elsewhere he sets out briefly some of the answers to this question:

> ... the causal chain extending from the command to the actual fact of compliance can be quite varied. Psychologically, the command may have achieved its effect upon the ruled either through empathy or through inspiration or through persuasion by rational argument or through some combination of these three principal types of influence of one person over another.[15]

Three broad types of compliance are here identified: empathy, inspiration, and susceptibility to rational argument. Had Weber chosen to pursue this line of thought he would perhaps have sought to show that there was likely to be a fair degree of symmetry between the three types of domination and the three types of compliance. In ideal-typical terms, traditional domination could be expected to elicit 'empathetic' compliance, charismatic domination could be expected to elicit 'inspirational' compliance, and legal-rational or bureaucratic domination could be expected to elicit 'rational' compliance. Since the character of compliance is to a large degree conditioned by the character of authority and command, some degree of affinity between the two could be anticipated. This would have opened up questions about deviations from the ideal-type in the shape of those authority systems in which a given type of domination co-existed with an 'inappropriate' type of compliance.[16]

Although questions along these lines might have highlighted some of the strains to be found in all structures of authority they would not have led to a comprehensive account of domination. Because Weber's three types of compliance are mirror images of his three types of domination they are still restricted to the narrow category of legitimate authority. Empathy, inspiration, and susceptibility to rational argument are simply different grounds on which subordinate groups accept commands as morally valid. Other answers to the question "When and why do men obey?" are still excluded by the terms of reference. Weber again hints at some of these other possible answers.

> In a concrete case the performance of a command may have been motivated by the ruled's own conviction of its propriety,

or by his sense of duty, or by fear, or by 'dull' custom, or by a desire to obtain some benefit for himself.[17]

This is a thumbnail sketch of a wider and much more useful typology of compliance. People obey orders (a) out of a sense of moral commitment ('propriety' and 'duty'); (b) out of sheer apathy or the inability to conceive alternative courses of action ('dull custom'); (c) out of fear of punishment; (d) through sheer expediency or self-interest. It is a pity that Weber did not expand upon this theme. Had he done so, he would have presented us with a classification of authority systems as viewed from below, not just from above. He could then have rounded off his analysis by setting up types of illegitimate domination as well. At the very least he would have been compelled to modify and tighten up his arguments concerning the extent of legitimate authority actually enjoyed by the men in command. A closer inspection of his three types of domination should make all this a little plainer.

III

Traditional domination. The most important form of traditional domination is patriarchalism and its offshoots. Weber says that the origins of patriarchalism are to be found in the master's authority over his household. The patriarch wields his power without legal restraints and unencumbered by formal rules. All that really circumscribes his authority over his subjects is the respect for sacred custom. Any master who repeatedly violated the boundaries etched by tradition would risk forfeiting his legitimacy. Obedience to the patriarchal master is based not on compliance with stated norms and codified procedures but on unquestioning personal loyalty, exemplified above all in the notion of filial piety.

Weber suggests that patriarchal domination always faces something of a crisis as soon as the master enlarges his domain and seeks to administer it along the same lines as the domestic unit. The patriarch generally gives responsibility for the oversee of his extended territories to his own direct dependents. For their part, the latter are always inclined to try to formalize and codify their duties and responsibilities towards the master and to specify their privileges and entitlements. The master will typically resist any such move since any formally prescribed rules would reduce the latitude of his purely discretionary and arbitrary powers. Patriarchs are willing to abide by custom but not conform to laws. Although the hallmark of patriarchal domination is said to be the voluntary submission of servants towards their master, it is clear from Weber's own account that the relationship is fraught with tension. Ruler and ruled are caught up in a subtle struggle for power, each party attempting to maintain or augment its own room for manoeuvre while ostensibly conforming to the imperatives of tradition.

Patrimonial domination, regarded by Weber as the commonest form of traditional domination, is in effect an extension of patriarchy. The basis of legitimacy is again the 'loyalty and fidelity' felt by subjects toward their master. Patrimonial rulers foster the same relationship with their political subjects that they enjoy with members of their household. While in theory they have absolute powers of command over their followers, in practice they are again held in check by the limits laid down by custom and convention. Weber sometimes argues that the conduct of patrimonial rulers is goverened and checked by their innate respect for the sanctity of tradition, and sometimes he argues that their self-restraint arises from prudential motives. An example of such motives is the master's recognition that his "omni-potence towards the individual dependent is paralleled by his power-lessness in face of the group."[18] If the patrimonial ruler uses his powers to excess, and in defiance of custom, he risks facing the collec-tive wrath of his nominally 'loyal' subjects. The unquestioning obe-dience that is said to be the bedrock of traditional domination looks as though it is very much conditional upon the ruler's good behaviour. Weber does in fact frequently make the point that the patrimonial ruler depends greatly on the goodwill of his subordinates. The loss of their goodwill would spell the end of his domination. This is not likely to occur as long as the subordinates are reaping sufficient benefits and satisfactions from the master's regime. The patrimonial ruler must thus see to it that his subjects are kept sweet by allowing them a share of his own booty, tax revenues and the spoils of war. What Weber presents as a moral or normative commitment on the part of the servants towards their master does in fact seem to be spiced with a fair measure of calculating self-interest.

The relationship between the patrimonial lord and his dependents and retainers becomes ever more strained as the territorial jurisdiction of the lord increases. The extension of the ruler's political authority, by way of conquest or whatever, calls for the devolution of responsi-bility into the hands of his chosen dependents. An administrative apparatus makes its appearance, subtly encroaching on the prerogatives of the lord and master. As the apparatus swells in size, more tax revenues are needed to feed it. The revenues that the administration was set up to collect are more and more swallowed up by the benifices enjoyed by the officials themselves.

Weber points out that patrimonial officialdom bears certain resemblances to bureaucracy, particularly in its functional division of tasks and hierarchy of command.[19] But the differences from bureaucracy are even more pronounced. To begin with, patrimonial administration knows no clear separation of private and official spheres. The ruler governs his political territory by personal fiat and draws upon wide discretionary powers. His officials are charged simply with the task of faithfully doing his bidding. There are none of the statutory practices and formal procedures of rational bureaucracy. The bureaucrat owes allegiance to the rules, never to a ruler. Furthermore the patrimonial official normally owned his benefice. He could sell his office or pass it on to his heirs just as though it were an item of private property. Administrative competence or technical ability were not important qualifications for office; fidelity to the ruler was the thing that counted above all else. Under this arrangement, the dispensation of justice was somewhat erratic.

> Instead of bureaucratic impartiality ... based on the abstract validity of one objective law for all ... the opposite principle prevails. Practically everything depends explicitly upon personal considerations: upon the attitude toward the concrete applicant and his concrete request and upon purely personal connections, favours, promises and privileges.[20]

Weber contrasts patrimonialism not only with bureaucracy but with another important sub-type of traditional domination — feudalism. Feudalism differed from patrimonialism in that the relationship between a lord and his vassals was a freely contractual one. The vassal swore fealty to his Lord and was no mere dependent. In addition, "Vassalage does not diminish the honour and status of the vassal; on the contrary, it can augment his honour ..."[21] The vassal identifies his fortune with that of his lord, and in the glory of his master he sees the reflection of himself. Most importantly, the vassal's claim to legitimacy *vis-à-vis* his own local subjects and dependents flowed directly from the legitimacy of the feudal lord.

The fact that the lord-vassal relationship was a reciprocal and contractual affair meant that rights and obligations were far more formalized under feudalism than under patrimonialism. Weber goes so far as to suggest that feudalism foreshadows, in a rather primitive form, the 'separation of powers' later developed by constitutional states.[22] The important difference was that feudal powers always inhered in persons not in offices. Individuals had no formal rights enshrined in law, only privileges granted by the grace of their lordly rulers.

It is noteworthy that Weber's account of traditional domination — patriarchal, patrimonial, and feudal — concerns itself mainly with the dealings between rulers and their immediate subordinates and officials. These men themselves, prebends, knights, barons, and the like, exercised considerable sway over large numbers of their own followers and underlings. Weber says remarkably little about the relationship between patrimonial or feudal lords and the ordinary masses, or even about the relationship between the masses and the lord's immediate lieutenants. The peasantry, on whose labour the entire edifice of patrimonialism rested, figure not at all in his analysis. The reader is left wondering how much devotion the average serf felt towards his lord and masters as they made their imperious demands for taxes and labour services.

Weber might have supposed, quite plausibly, that political cohesion in traditional societies depended in the main on good relations between various groups at the apex of society. Provided that the men on horseback did not fall out among themselves too badly the labouring people could be pacified without undue difficulty. Weber does indeed state that "a certain minimum of consent on the part of the ruled, at least of the *socially important strata*, is a precondition of every ... domination."[23] This does rather suggest that what the socially unimportant strata feel is a good deal less decisive. There is certainly little in the historical record to indicate that patrimonial or feudal authority was ever seriously dislocated by the murmuring of the masses or by bread riots or even by the occasional peasants' revolt. Because ruling elites in traditional societies always monopolized the means of violence, order could be preserved even if the many who shouldered the burden of production did *not* accept the legitimacy of the few who lived off the surplus.

Weber might well have been right in thinking that dominance and legitimacy in traditional societies were matters of relevance only among the topmost groups, and that it was therefore permissible to disregard the relationship between elites and masses. But he would have done well to make this point explicit. His accounts of feudalism and patrimonialism suggest, misleadingly, that legitimate domination is the governing principle running through the entire society, not just its upper crust. Unlike the stance he adopts in his sociology of religion, there is no readiness to explore the possibility of an 'elective affinity' between a group's willingness to accept its ruler's claims to legitimacy and its own place in a rigidly stratified system.

IV

Charismatic domination. Weber counterposes charismatic domination to both traditional and legal-rational or bureaucratic domination. Although patrimonialism and bureaucracy differ from one another in most respects, they do have one important thing in common: they are both formal and lasting structures that are geared to the routines of mundane life. Bureaucracy could, in this respect at least, be looked upon as the rational counterpart of traditional authority.[24] Domination that arises on the basis of charisma is altogether different from either of these other types because it lacks all forms of established organization. Charisma relies upon no hierarchy of office, salaried employees, technical administration or procedural rules of any kind. Whereas bureaucracy and patrimonial administration need to be sustained by money revenues received on a regular and reliable footing, charisma spurns all methodical rational acquisition as morally degrading. In place of routine economic activity the charismatic leader and his disciples rely for their subsistence upon gifts, voluntary donations or booty. All other types of domination and political rule abhor a hand to mouth existence; charismatic leadership thrives on it.

The authority of the charismatic leader is dependent solely upon his ability to convince his followers and disciples of his extraordinary powers. He must perform miracles and heroic deeds, and continually prove his divine mission in the eyes of his followers. Unlike the bureaucrat he cannot rest on the security of office; unlike the patriarch he cannot take refuge in the sanctity of custom. He must always be ready to demonstrate his gifts by awe-inspiring acts or risk forfeiting the faith of his disciples. Like the modern sporting hero, his performance is kept under perpetual review by his adulators. Repeated failure leads to disillusionment and the quick evaporation of his following.

Charisma is thus very different from Weber's other two types of legitimate domination. Indeed, there is a case for saying that charismatic legitimacy is the only pure type of legitimacy. The charismatic leader has no sway over his followers and disciples other than the faith that they voluntarily invest in him. When they cease to believe in him his authority is immediately annulled. The litmus test of genuine legitimacy is whether or not subordinates are willing to obey the master's commands when he has no power to punish recalcitrants. If the leader's authority is backed up, ultimately, by recourse to physical or material sanctions, the motives for obedience are likely to be much more complex than a straightforward belief in his legitimacy. In the case of traditional domination, for example, the subjects of the patrimonial master are perfectly well aware that their refusal to comply with his commands is likely to result in the use of quite robust methods to encourage them to think again. Similarly with legal-rational domination. Weber suggests that under this type of domination obedience is given not to persons but to rules that are regarded as morally binding. People comply with the laws because they regard them as 'valid'. Once again, though, it is not easy to be sure how far such laws are obeyed simply out of recognition of their legitimacy when it is perfectly well known that any infraction could result in a visit from large men in blue uniforms.

Weber makes no separation between legitimacy that is contaminated by fear of sanctions and that which is not. His account of the legitimacy that flows from charisma highlights the shortcomings of treating other types of domination as comparable cases of legitimate authority. Only the charismatic leader must rely upon the purely voluntary compliance of his followers; they are free to spurn his commands wherever they wish, without any serious comeback. The patrimonial lord and the bureacrat would no doubt prefer it if their commands were also obeyed out of a sense of love, admiration and respect for their person or their office. It would be nice for them to know that their popular legitimacy was so secure that they had no need to threaten or cajole. But as things stand, they are wise enough not to rely too much on voluntary compliance. The legitimacy of charisma, by contrast, rests wholly upon the faith invested in the leader, and faith cannot be coerced. Under all other forms of domination, compliance with the master's commands is animated by knowledge of the consequences that non-compliance may bring.

The fact that charismatic leadership eschews coercion means that, unlike traditionalism and bureaucracy, it cannot be the basis of a stable system of political rule. No sooner does charisma come into being than the process of its decline begins. Weber points out that charismatic gifts are in demand during periods of unrest and common excitation, but that such gifts are not well suited to the management of humdrum affairs. Charismatics love a crisis, but they cannot cope with the routine demands of getting and spending that every social order must attend to. The ordinary business of the state cannot wait upon the inspiration of the leader and his wondrous deeds; and any permanent regime will need to rely on more than its citizens' faith in the great man to win obedience to its rules. But the very attempt to routinize charisma, to tame it and harness it to the service of mundane ends, leads only to its dissipation. Because charisma is a gift that inheres in the extraordinary, once-in-a-lifetime individual, it cannot be preserved and passed on. After the death of the charismatic leader there is a crisis of succession that can never be properly resolved. With the appointment of a successor things are never quite the same. Charisma is thus a flame that burns with a bright intensity for a short while and is then suddenly extinguished. In the aftermath of charismatic rule, authority reverts either to a more traditional mould or starts to take on bureaucratic features.

Weber makes it clear that no evolutionary pattern of development is discernible in all this. Societies do not pass through a sequence of traditional, charismatic, and legal-rational stages. All three types of domination occur in various combinations throughout different periods of history.[25] What does happen, though, is that the impact of charisma on the social order tends to become weaker once bureaucracy has thoroughly taken root. Weber considered charisma to be a powerfully disruptive force on all established orders; it was the "specifically creative revolutionary force of history."[26] Traditional societies were especially vulnerable to the shock-waves of charisma. Wherever people were embalmed in the orthodoxies of custom and habit, the charismatic figure rising up from nowhere could wreak havoc on the old order.

While Weber did not generally subscribe to a 'great man' theory of history, the equation of charisma with revolutionary powers does seem to cast unique individuals in the most glamorous role in historical dramas. He does, however, add that bureaucracies can be revolutionary too, in the scale and manner in which they have often transformed patrimonial and other traditional societies. The difference between the two kinds of revolutionary force is that bureaucracy transforms from 'without' whereas charisma works its magic from 'within'.[27] That is to say, bureaucracy alters social and economic institutions, while charisma brings about a transfiguration of the self. Those who fall under the spell of charisma are re-made into entirely new people.

Societies in which legal-rational domination was the norm might be less vulnerable to the disturbances of charisma but they were by no means immune from them. In any social order there would always be enough suffering or simmering rage or cosmic anxiety to ensure a following for the leader with a simple solution to it all. Occasionally, Weber thought of charisma as the one force that was capable of transcending the dreary constraints of bureaucratic life. Charisma had wings and could fly through the bars of the iron cage. At other times he felt that bureaucracy was more than a match for the charismatic firebrand. In the hurly-burly of party politics, for example, "Only extraordinary conditions can bring about the triumph of charisma over the organization."[28] In the usual course of events the bureaucratic party machine would see to it that the "castration of charisma" was performed swiftly and efficiently.[29]

The extraordinary conditions that encouraged the eruption of charisma in bureaucratic or traditional settings could not be clearly specified in advance. The fact that Weber did not spell out the circumstances which led to the rise of a messiah or an Ayatollah has provoked the complaint that he had no 'theory of revolution'.[30] While this is true it somewhat misses the point. The striking thing about charisma is its complete unpredictability. It can break out in the least expected times and places. Events brought on by such a mercurial force do not lend themselves to easy generalization. In any case, not to have had a theory of revolution hardly warrants a black mark, especially when it is borne in mind that most such 'theories' turn out to be little more than demonstrations of wisdom after the event. Theorists of revolution are very good at predicting the past. Since the timely appearance of an inspired leader is usually considered to be a necessary ingredient of revolution, and since chance and accident play an important part in this, the element of unpredictability in the shape of charisma would seem to bedevil any attempt to go beyond the vaguest of general statements about the causes of revolution.

It has already been said that Weber thought the revolutionary potential of charisma would be much reduced with the onset of bureaucratic rationality. "It is the fate of charisma ... to recede with the development of permanent institutional structures."[31] Charisma might continue to erupt in a small way in this or that rational organization, or to flourish in the interstices of the body bureaucratic; but it would be unlikely to turn the entire society upside down. In a fully rational and secularized society the appeal of the charismatic prophet would perhaps be confined to gilded youth in search of identity and keen to .embark on voyages of the mind. Weber would have been unsurprised at the spectacle of the sons and daughters of the modern bourgeoisie held in thrall by chubby mystics from the East. He might, though, have been more surprised, as well as deeply shocked, at the apparent ease with which a charismatic leader on his own doorstep would revolutionize an entire society and bend its rational structures to the most devastatingly irrational purposes. Within a decade or so of Weber's death, charisma was shown to be anything but a spent force.

V

Legal-rational domination. The typical form of this type of domination is bureaucracy. "In a modern state", Weber says, "the actual ruler is necessarily and unavoidably the bureaucracy ..."[32] Under all other types of domination authority resides in persons — patriarch and lord, messiah and revolutionary leader. Under bureaucracy alone authority is vested in rules; it is a system of laws not of men. The hallmark of bureaucratic domination is its studied impartiality. Its officials act without prejudice or passion, applying the same rules to all irrespective of differences in social rank and condition. The bureaucrat, moreover, is not the ultimate fount of rule. Unlike the traditional or charismatic leader, the official in the modern state is himself the servant of a higher political authority — typically an elected government and its ministers. Willing obedience is thus a necessary attribute of the good bureaucrat.

The trouble is that bureaucrats do not always behave in the way they are supposed to. They have an understandable human tendency to try and accrue power for themselves, and to push their own private interests. Instead of behaving as faithful servants they seek to become masters in their own house. Weber was very much exercised by the problem of how to ensure that the state bureaucracy was kept in its proper place by the elected representatives of the people. The civil service might be admirably equipped to perform its administrative duties, but it could not and should not be entrusted with matters of high policy. This was the business of parliament and the politicians. A good politician thrives on controversy and the cut and thrust of debate; the bureaucrat is unfitted for such matters and has a responsibility to stand aloof from party squabbles. While it is right and proper for the high bureaucrat to advise his minister, and even to present a reasoned case, he is duty bound to accept the minister's decision and to implement it as conscientiously as though it corresponded to his own innermost conviction.[33]

Weber argued that bureaucracy had a telling advantage over the elected politician in that it held close and jealous control over the means of information. Secrecy and monopoly of the files were handy weapons at the disposal of every bureaucracy. Then as now "... bureaucracy's supreme power instrument is the transformation of official information into classified material ..."[34] By the careful manipulation of evidence and the selective presentation of facts, bureaucrats could dictate or strongly influence policy under the guise of administrative impartiality. Government ministers were always in danger of becoming little more than ventriloquists' dummies of their own departmental servants.

It is significant that Weber considers this sort of behaviour by the bureaucracy to be thoroughly reprehensible. His biting comments on the arrogance of the German civil service in its dealings with parliament make it clear that he saw the intrusion of bureaucracy into the political sphere as an abuse of power. The bureaucracy was attempting to usurp the authority of government. This presents something of a problem for his typology of legitimate domination. If bureaucracy acts in strict accordance with the rules of legal-rational authority it necessarily places itself in a subordinate position to a higher body. Technically, bureaucrats are always the servants and never the masters. That being so, it is difficult to see why bureaucracy should qualify as a type of 'domination'. It makes sense to regard traditional or charismatic leaders as dominant authorities because nobody is entitled to tell them what to do. Someone is always expected to tell the bureaucrats what to do. If bureaucracy does attempt to exercise domination it usurps the authority of a nominally superior body. In other words it uses its power illegitimately. Thus, in the light of Weber's own account, bureaucracy can hardly be an example of 'legitimate domination'. If it acts legitimately it is not dominant; if it exercises domination it ceases to be legitimate.

4

Class, Status, and Party

I

In his brief and celebrated treatise on social stratification Weber identifies three "phenomena of the distribution of power within a community": *classes, status groups* and *parties*.[1] Each of these represents a distinct aspect of power in so far as each constitutes a different basis for staking claims to material and symbolic rewards. The three dimensions or phenomena of power are said to stand in some definite relationship to one another in the stratification order. But when it comes down to it, Weber is much more concerned with the relationship between class and status than with the link between either of these and party. Party proves to be very much the odd man out.

One of the most immediately noteworthy things about this initial classification is what it leaves out. Among possible candidates for inclusion in the catalogue of power, the state and bureaucracy stand out as distinguished absentees. This is mildly surprising in view of the importance these are generally accorded in Weber's political sociology. As we have already seen, he often seems to regard state and bureaucracy as among the heavyweights in the struggle for power. To call the modern state an agency that successfully claims a monopoly of the use of physical force within a territorial community is clearly to speak of the exercise of power of the most extreme kind. Bureaucracy, too, is generally looked upon as an immense source of power, potential or actual, and one that is quite different from the power that flows from the possession of economic trappings and resources. To be perfectly fair, Weber does not say that classes, status groups and parties are the *only* phenomena of power in a community; but the fact that he singles these out for attention does suggest that he felt them to be of unusual importance. Let us examine each of them in turn.

In his discussion of social class Weber takes a leaf out of Marx's book by according special priority to the role of private property. Throughout his writings he makes the point that property or productive wealth heaps many benefits and prerogatives upon its possessors, while those who must rely on selling their labour are severely handicapped in the struggle for resources. "'Property' and 'lack of property' are, therefore, the basic categories of all class situations."[2] Weber certainly did not subscribe to the classical liberal doctrine of the natural harmony of interests between capital and labour. The relationship between the two was not one of mutual reciprocity; it was one of profound inequality in which capital definitely had the upper hand.

> The formal right of a worker to enter into any contract whatsoever with any employer whatsoever does not in practice represent for the employment seeker even the slightest freedom in the determination of his own conditions of work, and it does not guarantee him any influence in this process. It rather means ... that the more powerful party in the market, i.e. normally the employer, has the possibility to set the terms, to offer the job, 'take it or leave it', and, given the normally more pressing economic need of the worker, to impose his own terms upon him.[3]

The freedom of contract was thus the freedom of the property owner to exploit the worker. To speak, as Weber does, of the 'wage whip' that keeps the worker in line is clearly not the language of Adam Smith and his latter day acolytes. For Weber, as for Marx, the relationship between propertied and propertyless classes was inherently conflictual, something that was part of the very fabric of capitalism. Unlike Marx, however, Weber did not seem to regard this as either remediable or altogether heinous. Conflict over the distribution of resources was a natural feature of any type of society and to imagine an earthly paradise of harmony and equality was pie in the sky. Property was but one source of divisiveness and mischief among men and its abolition would be followed by other equally malevolent substitutes.

Weber's assertion that class relations are founded upon property relations appears at first blush to be contradicted by certain of his other claims. He denies, for example, that there is anything all that unusual about the worker's lack of ownership of the means of production. The bureaucrat does not own the means of administration, the military man does not own the means of destruction, and so on. The absence of formal property rights was not much of a hindrance to the monopolization and control of worldly goods. You could grow rich and fat and powerful without actually owning anything. Weber's essay on bureaucracy could easily be read as a counterblast against the proposition that private property was the root of all social, economic and political power. Surely one of the main purposes of that treatise was to show that power could be wielded, and men and things controlled, by those whose authority was vested in office 'Lack of property' hardly seems to be a serious drawback to the life-chances of Weber's typical bureaucrat.

If bureaucracy could dispose over the allocation of resources without benefit of ownership why should Weber so readily have agreed with Marx that class relations went hand in hand with property relations? The short answer seems to be that he did not regard bureaucracy as akin to a social class. Social classes arose only in response to two related conditions — property ownership and the sale of labour service in the marketplace. Where the distributive system rested on something other than private property and market forces, social classes could not exist. "According to our terminology, the factor that creates 'class' is unambiguously economic interest, and indeed, only those interests involved in the existence of the market". Hence, those groups and collectivities

> whose fate is not determined by the chance of using goods or services for themselves on the market, e.g. slaves, are not . . . a class in the technical sense of the term. They are, rather, a status group.[4]

For Weber, then, the history of all hitherto existing societies was not the history of class struggle. Struggle could be just as intense between groups other than social classes. Slavery and bureaucracy were forms of domination that owed little to the free play of those market forces and contractual relations that were so necessary for the domination of one class by another. One implication of this argument would seem to be that contemporary socialist states, having done away with private property and the market, would have to be thought of as classless societies. Weber would presumably have been prepared to endorse Trotsky's view that Soviet-style bureaucracies were not dominant or exploiting classes, notwithstanding the immense power and privileges they enjoyed. Weber could in fact have defended this proposition more happily than Trotsky since he gave every indication of believing that bureaucratic domination under socialism would be far nastier than mere class domination under capitalism. The classless society was more of a nightmare than a dream.[5]

When social class is defined in such close association with the conditions of the marketplace, a problem arises in the attempt to show where one class ends and another one begins. There is obviously a very wide range of market situations stemming from the modern division of labour. Those who sell their labour power may be advantaged and disadvantaged in many different kinds of ways. Some groups will be able to lay claim to rewards on the basis of their special skills or paper qualifications, others may derive bargaining power from the strategic position they occupy in the production process. The marketplace is an arena in which all occupational groups are indirectly in contention with each other. Each seeks to maximize its share of a finite cake; more for some means less for others. The model or image that is conjured up by these activities is of a society fragmented into innumerable divisions and subdivisions, not of a society split between a dominant and a subordinate class.

Weber declares that classes are composed of the various groups whose market opportunities and life-chances are broadly similar. But there is no clear-cut way of identifying notional boundaries that mark off different segments of the reward hierarchy from one another, and hence no way of settling the problem of the number of classes actually in play. It is thus quite understandable that many theorists working within the Weberian tradition should have opted for a classless model of the stratification system and jettisoned altogether the imagery of class domination and class subjection in favour of a generalized notion of social inequality.

Although Weber himself preferred to use the vocabulary of class he never formulated a clear and systematic model of class. In his macro-social and comparative studies he frequently employs Marx's familiar categories of class: aristocracy, peasantry, bourgeoisie, proletariat. But in his analysis of capitalist society he never makes altogether plain the formal criteria by which bourgeoisie and proletariat are to be distinguished from one another. For Marx the issue was fairly straightforward; the bourgeoisie was defined by its ownership of the means of production, the proletariat by its need to sell labour power. The two great classes of capital and labour were thus conceived of as formal attributes of the capitalist system, not as two composite bodies made up of various groups having certain social characteristics in common.

Weber could reject this neat and tidy formulation by pointing out that in Marx's schema 'labour' was a catch-all category that encompassed too many diverse conditions of employment to be called a class. It would be a funny-looking proletariat, he implied, that included among its ranks lawyers and coalminers, doctors and dustmen, managers and truck drivers. Having paid lip-service to Marx's proposition that lack of property was the basic determinant of the working class, Weber then proceeds to undermine it by developing the theme of market differentiation and conflict among the multitudes who sell their labour. Stratification within the marketplace virtually dissolves the proletariat as a class.

Having in effect abandoned the distinction between capital and labour as the defining elements of class, Weber never proposes an alternative model. That is, he sets out no principles by which to locate the notional 'boundary' between a dominant or exploiting class and a subordinate or exploited class. What is portrayed instead is a Hobbesian war of all against all as each group fights its own corner in the anarchy of the marketplace. Now, that might of course be a closer approximation to the way things really are than is any simple, dichtomous model of class − be it Marxist or any other. There is no shortage of sociologists willing to argue that the complexities of a modern capitalist society cannot be captured by a procrustean model of class, and that 'social differentiation' is the more useful and appropriate construct to employ. The fact is, however, that Weber himself preferred to use the moral vocabulary of class and class conflict, even though he offered no solution of his own to the 'boundary problem'.

There is another feature of Weber's account of stratification that tends to play down the importance of property ownership. This is the priority that he generally accords to the distributive system over the productive system. It is this shift in priorities that most Marxists would regard as the really crucial difference between their own approach and a Weberian one. The standard Marxist assumption is that the mode of production is the governing element in the entire social system. Directly or indirectly it sets its stamp upon all other leading social activities and formations, including the distributive system. Weber is therefore held to be in grievous error in so far as his attention is directed to the wrong level of reality. He is concerned with the world of mere appearances − patterns of social inequality and distribution − instead of with the real essence of things, the system of productive relations. In short, Weber is accused of a preoccupation with social effects or consequences, rather than with their underlying causes.

Weber was not too impressed by the claim that the mode of production always created the structure of social inequality in its own image. Any given type of productive system could co-exist with a variety of different stratification systems. According to Marx, "The hand mill gives you society with the feudal lord; the steam mill, society with the industrial capitalist."[6] Weber's rejoinder to this was that the steam mill could just as easily give you a socialist society as a capitalist one. Moreover, the "hand-mill has lived through all conceivable economic structures and political 'superstructures'." The historically common system of patrimonialism was "compatible with household and market economy, petty-bourgeois and manorial agriculture, absence and presence of capitalist economy."[7] The mode of production by no means had the decisive, or even the final, say in the shape of other social formations.

To speak of productive systems in terms of hand mills and steam mills is a rather quaint technological usage that has long since passed out of fashion. Yet even if a broader meaning is employed, Weber's argument still retains its force. If, for example, a socialist mode of production is thought of as one in which property has been collectivized and the free market has been replaced by central planning, quite different political and social arrangements can be seen to arise on this same foundation. China in the epoch of the Cultural Revolution was stratified along different lines from the Soviet Union under Stalin. Albania and Poland, North Korea and Cuba, Kampuchea and Yugoslavia, differ sufficiently in their systems of reward and punishment to cast grave doubt on the belief that patterns of distribution can somehow be 'read off' from the mode of production.

This is even more so in the case of the capitalist mode of production, not least of all because of the greater political leeway that is generally allowed to competing interest groups to mobilize in pursuit of their ends. Weber placed much emphasis on the fact that conflicting interest groups were not necessarily class formations. Equally important were those collectivities inspired by a sense of their 'communal' identity — be it racial, religious, linguistic or whatever. He was a lot more sensitive than Marx to social formations arising on the basis of these ethnic and cultural divisions in society. Social inequalities and conflicts between communal groups could not very easily be laid at the door of the capitalist mode of production. They were endemic in every known type of society, past and present, whatever the way it handled its productive affairs.

In Weber's presentation, the factors that account for stratification along ethnic or racial lines are largely the outcome of historical contingency. The reasons why one society was divided along religious lines, another along racial lines, and yet another along language lines, could no doubt be made intelligible in each particular case. But to offer an historical account of how these things came about did not call for the aid of some grand 'theory' that purported to explain it all. Weber was clearly sceptical that any general theory of this kind could possibly cope with such diversity and complexity. Certainly the primitive ideas contained in Historical Materialism were not up to the task.

Weber's way of looking at the problem would seem to imply a reversal of the causal sequence proposed by Marx and his followers. Instead of treating the mode of production as a kind of governing body to the rest of society, it is looked upon as having a more accommodating role. It can be shown to adapt itself to existing social arrangements rather than bending them to its own design. The capitalist mode of production, for example, would appear to show a great deal of flexibility in conforming to the contours of ethnic and communal cleavages; it is less active than acted upon by existing forms of social stratification.[8] Weber would be able to point out that the record of the capitalist mode of production in liquidating ethnic and other tribal divisions in the modern industrial state was none too impressive.

II

Communal divisions are among the most important examples of status groups, the second of Weber's three phenomena of the distribution of power. In his discussion of status or social honour he points out that the distribution of this symbolic reward did not always correspond to the distribution of material reward. In the long run, status privileges did tend to go hand in hand with private wealth, if only because the pursuit of an elevated style of life was a continuous drain on the purse. But at any given time there was often likely to be some discrepancy between the material standing of a social group and its place in the hierarchy of esteem. Impoverished Brahmins and down-at-heel aristocrats could confidently expect to be deferred to by others better off then themselves, while men of new wealth were generally looked down upon by families of breeding and pedigree. Moreover, even where wealth and social honour were roughly on a par, the relationship between them was not always in the same causal direction. Sometimes social honour flowed from material possessions, sometimes it was more like a springboard to the attainment of such possessions.

Disjunctions between class position and status position were especially liable to occur under capitalism. This was because capitalist market relations are governed by purely impersonal considerations. The market, as Weber puts it, "knows nothing of honour".

> The status order means precisely the reverse: stratification in terms of honour and styles of life peculiar to status groups as such. The status order would be threatened at its very root if mere economic acquisition and naked economic power still bearing the stigma of its extra-status origin could bestow upon anyone who has won them the same or even greater honour as the vested interests claim for themselves.[9]

Weber tended to see status groups as fairly combative bodies. And in this respect his work is at some odds with that of many of his intellectual descendants. Among the latter, status groups are often thought of as being concerned almost exclusively with the intangibles of honour and prestige; they are thus set in sharp contrast to social classes, which are openly geared to the pursuit of material ends. Seen from this perspective, trade unions are held to be class organizations because of their commitment to bread-and-butter goals, while professional associations are held to be status organizations because of the priority they allegedly give to the preservation of their members' good standing in the eyes of the community. Classes and status groups are thus differentiated not only in terms of their social bases but also according to the kinds of ends they seek.[10]

There is not much warrant for this view in Weber's work. He presents status groups as collectivities that mobilize their members for competitive struggles of all kinds, material and symbolic. That is, they act in a manner not too dissimilar from that of social classes or the organizations based on social classes. "For all practical purposes stratification by status goes hand in hand with a monopolization of ideal and material goods or opportunities ..."[11] The fact that status groups are not the same as social classes does not prevent them from engaging in distributive struggle. Indeed, Weber occasionally drops a hint that they may sometimes be more effective in this respect than social classes. The problem with classes is that they are too heterogeneous and internally divided to act as a concerted force for any length of time. There is in fact something rather improbable about the notion of a social class being cast in the role of a social actor. Status groups, on the other hand, are generally moral communities. They are more likely to have a powerful sense of their own common identity and of the social boundary separating them off from others, especially if there is a racial, religious or ethnic component present. As a consequence they can be more readily mobilized for collective ends.[12]

Weber's introduction of the notion of status and status groups into stratification theory was intended to serve as an antidote to pure class analysis. It served, in particular, to cast doubt upon Marx's thesis of class polarization. This thesis proposed that the two great classes of history would become increasingly homogeneous as the crisis of capitalism intensified. The middle ground between bourgeoisie and proletariat would become politically uninhabitable and they would eventually confront one another as two armed camps. Weber's analysis suggested a different outcome. Status groups within each of the main classes would forestall any move in the direction of internal unity and coherence. As the division of labour became more complex, classes became more rather than less heterogeneous. As usual, Weber's eye was caught by the factors that tended to dissolve the solidarities of class, both in the marketplace and in the status order. Given the irreversible effect of these corrosive forces, the chances of class confrontation on the grand scale were reckoned to be extremely slim.

Status group formations that work against the unification of class are of two different kinds, though Weber does not treat them as such. There are status groups that arise *within* social classes and those that *cut across* social classes. Status groups that arise within a social class are generally rooted in the division of labour or the property system. These are the sorts of groups that Marx occasionally alludes to. Within the bourgeoisie, for example, he points out the differences between finance capitalists and industrial capitalists, and suggests that their immediate interests may often be mutually incompatible. Lower down the system, he contrasts the position of white collar groups engaged in productive labour with the position of those engaged in unproductive labour. Finally, at the base of society, he distinguishes between the working class proper and the lumpenproletariat. Weber often refers to status groups of this kind, too, as, for example, when he contrasts the *rentier* element within the bourgeoisie with the entrepreneurial element.

Status groups that cut across classes are quite different; they are not creations of the division of labour or the productive system. The most important of these are the communal groupings already referred to and which feature in most societies, including modern capitalist and socialist societies. Marx paid much less attention to these status groups, believing as he did that such archaic survivals would be swept aside by the brutal progress of capitalism. As it turns out, however, it is precisely these status groups that have proved to be more enduring, while those nternal to the proletariat and bourgeoisie have become somewhat attenuated over time. Continuous changes in the division of labour and the disturbances of the market have undermined the traditional status order of the occupational system, much as Weber assumed they would. By contrast, communal status groups that cut across class lines show no such signs of diminishing — rather the reverse. They draw upon sentiments and identities that owe little to the vagaries of the division of labour, and their impediment to pure class formation and action is likely to be all the more formidable for it.

Weber points out that status groups of ethnic provenance derive their sense of social honour from sources that are largely independent of the formal structure of esteem and deference. The status order of the wider society is always a hierarchy of rank in which each group has its allotted place. In this officially sanctioned scheme of things there is not much opportunity for socially despised groups to have a much better opinion of themselves than the rest of the community has of them. The lowly are thus often inclined to accept the claims for deference made upon them by others of higher standing.

Ethnic status, Weber suggests, does not conform to this pattern. Every communal group tends to construct a sense of its own unique ethnic honour' that is immune from the denigration of outsiders. As a result, the various ethnic groups within a community do not become systematically ranked in a status hierarchy that is accepted by all. Each group jealously preserves and cultivates a sense of its own moral worth and dignity and of the inferiority of all other groups. Weber thus considers ethnic honour to be a "specific honour of the masses" because it is a source of self-esteem available to every member of the communal group, however humble his rank in the division of labour and the formal status order based upon it.[13]

Weber sometimes thinks of status groups as agencies of collective action that serve as alternatives to class-oriented action. The choice between status group and class activity would always to some extent be dictated by the nature of the goals being pursued; but the condition and temper of the times would also have a part to play. When society is in upheaval different strategies are called for from when a more tranquil mood prevails.

> When the bases of the acquisition and distribution of goods are relatively stable, stratification by status is favoured. Every technological repercussion and economic transformation threatens stratification by status and pushes the class situation into the foreground. Epochs and countries in which the naked

class situation is of predominant significance are regularly the periods of technical and economic transformations. And every slowing down of the change in economic stratification leads, in due course, to the growth of status structures and makes for a resuscitation of the important role of social honour.[14]

This proposition would seem to have fairly limited historical validity. Class conflict in the nineteenth and early twentieth centuries was no doubt sufficiently acute and absorbing as to force most other social question into the background. Class action during this period was aimed not merely at a more just distribution of goods and opportunities but at the incorporation of the propertyless masses into civil society. When the conflict between classes revolves upon issues as large as the political transformation of society it might well be that all status group demands pale into insignificance. But when class conflict becomes domesticated and routinized there is more social leeway for the furtherance of both class and status ambitions. Under modern capitalism, conflicts on the class and status fronts seem able to co-exist quite happily. In the present depths of industrial gloom and depression the heightened class activities that Weber would have predicted have been accompanied by a resurgence of ethnic group demands that he would not have predicted. Class and status group concerns do not, it seems, simply alternate with changes in the economic climate.

The manner in which status groups seek to mobilize power in a similar way to class organizations is revealed most clearly in Weber's discussion of social closure.[15] By social closure he means the process by which various groups attempt to improve their lot by restricting access to rewards and privileges to a limited circle. In order to do this they single out certain social or physical attributes that they themselves possess and define these as the criteria of eligibility. Weber says that almost any characteristic may be used to this end provided it can serve as a means of identifying and excluding 'outsiders'. "It does not matter which characteristic is chosen in the individual case; whatever suggests itself most easily is seized upon."[16] Exclusionary social closure is thus action by a status group designed to secure for itself certain resources and advantages at the expense of other groups. Where the excluded themselves manage to close off access to remaining rewards to other groups, the number of strata or sub-strata multiplies — as exemplified in the extreme case by the caste system.

The most effective and complete forms of social closure are those which employ criteria of descent and lineage, the criteria generally used by dominant groups in all traditional societies. In modern industrial societies, by contrast, closure is effected less by reference to family pedigree than by the use of devices such as tests and examinations that are ostensibly open and fair to all, irrespective of birth and family. Weber saw the educational system as an especially refined instrument for guarding and controlling entry to the charmed circles. Paper qualifications and certificates were almost as effective as lineage or skin colour or religion as a means of monitoring the entry of the chosen few into the greener pastures. So:

> If we hear from all sides demands for the introduction of regulated curricula culminating in specialized examinations, the reason behind this is, of course, not a suddenly awakened 'thirst for education', but rather the desire to limit the supply of candidates for these positions and to monpololize them for the holders of educational patents. For such monopolization, the 'examination' is today the universal instrument — hence its irresistible advance.[17]

In addition to controlling and screening entrants by way of examinations, the best rewarded professional groups try to win for themselves certain legal privileges. They attempt to enlist the support of the state in winning exclusive rights to perform their tasks and bringing punishment on the heads of those who infringe their monopoly. In this way an occupational status group is able to enjoy considerable protection from the hazards of open competition in the marketplace. Groups that fail to bring about complete social closure with legal backing are usually unable to establish a monopoly or to retain full control over the selection and training of new members.

Weber's comment about legal monopolies is practically the only reference he makes to the role of the state in the closure process, or indeed in the stratification system in general. The struggles between different classes or status groups, and collective efforts to bring about social closure, are events that take place on the terrain of civil society. Social groups confront one another as competitors and antagonists in the marketplace, handicapped or advantaged by virtue of their own possessions, skills and attributes. The state is a shadowy body that hardly intrudes upon the scene. This is very strange in a way because Weber certainly never thought of the state as an agency that was 'above' society, an impartial umpire adjudicating between the warring factions below. He himself had argued that the laws upholding private property and market relations worked mainly to the advantage of those who had managed to get such laws enacted. The state backed up these laws with all the awesome means at its disposal. But for some mysterious reason the state does not qualify as one of the phenomena of the distribution of power.

This leads to a serious flaw in Weber's account of social closure. In discussing the criteria employed by different groups to exclude others from goods and opportunities he claims that any attribute or characteristic will do: "whatever suggests itself most easily is seized upon".[18] But obviously this cannot be so. It is *never* the case that exclusionary criteria are simply plucked out of thin air in a purely arbitrary fashion. In all known instances where lineage or race or religion or sex or similar features have been seized upon for closure purposes the excluded group has already at some time been defined as inferior by the state. Racial and ethnic closure, to take the commonest case, has normally followed in the wake of colonial conquest or the forced migration of populations, creating a sub-category of second class citizens within the boundaries of the nation state. The communities singled out for exclusion — blacks, Catholics, Jews or other minorities — are typically those whose political and social rights have been deliberately curtailed by the forces of law and order. Such groups become the target for exclusionary practices precisely because their capacity to resist has been undermined by the state powers. If it were merely a matter of one group 'seizing upon' some convenient attribute or other, it should in theory have been possible for Catholics in Northern Ireland to exclude Protestants from jobs and housing, instead of the reverse; blacks in the Deep South should have been able to seize upon white skin colour as a criterion of exclusion; it should have been within the ability of women to close off life-chances and opportunities to men, and so on. None of these possibilities could in fact be realised because the state had not already prepared the way for closure along these lines.

By disregarding the role of the state in internal affairs Weber is unable to offer a coherent account of the way in which social and status differentiation becomes crystallized into a system of structured inequality. The principles by which classes, status groups and strata are ranked and rewarded in relation to each other are guaranteed and enforced by the ultimate authority in the land. Privileges that the state confers can also be withdrawn, meaning that it is in the power of the state to alter or re-shape the stratification order. There is little in Weber's account that would alert us to the fact that the balance of advantages between different classes or strata could be changed in ways that mattered by the determined intervention of the central powers. Without some form of state power, however rudimentary, a stratified system could hardly exist.

Weber's unwillingness to conceive of the state as an instrumental agency in the distributive system might possibly have been because he shared Marx's view of the state as something that was less active than acted upon. The bourgeois state, at least, was thought of by Marx as a kind of arena in which class struggles were given formal political expression. The most powerful class in civil society would naturally control the levers of state authority and hence make its dominance secure. Looked at from this angle, the state apparatus was akin to a machine that could be put to the service of any body that was socially and economically powerful enough to take command of it. The state reinforced and legitimated the power of such a body, it did not create it *de novo*. Given these fairly limited functions there would not be much point in looking at the state as a redistributive agency in its own right.

Weber goes along with this argument part of the way. He certainly accepted the view of the state as an instrument waiting to be wielded by any group or class able to grasp hold of it. A bureaucratic state apparatus

> is easily made to work for anybody who knows how to gain control over it. A rationally ordered officialdom continues to function smoothly after the enemy has occupied the territory: he merely needs to change the top officials.[19]

Although Weber saw the state as a powerful tool in the hands of a class or status group he did not subscribe to Marx's view of it as an 'executive committee' of the bourgeoisie. There were two reasons for this:

Firstly, he was acutely aware from the German experience that the capitalist state was not inevitably under the control of the bourgeoisie. One of the structural flaws in German society, as he saw it, was that state power was monopolized not by the capitalist entrepreneurial class but by the Junker aristocracy. Internal contradictions arose from the fact that an economically backward and politically moribund class occupied the seat of power, while the bourgeoisie (the rightful heirs?) made no real effort to take charge. The trouble with the German state was that it was the executive committee of the wrong social class.[20]

Secondly, Weber sometimes thought of the state bureaucratic machine less as an instrument for someone else's use than as a collectivity with values, aims and purposes of its own. The special ethos and *esprit de corps* within the bureaucracy, its cultivation of secrecy and professional craftiness, made it a formidable interest group in its own right. It acted not as an executive committee of another class but as an organized status group out to feather its own nest. While not itself being a class, in the technical sense, it could nevertheless vie with the power of social classes on practically equal terms.

Bureaucracy was thus, in effect, the most powerful of all status groups. It held sway over the disposition of men and resources without benefit of property ownership or market monopolies. Weber's insistence that bureaucratic power could arise independently of the power of social classes compounded the differences between his own theoretical outlook on stratification and that of Marxism. Marxism is not at all happy with the idea that power can emerge in society alongside and separate from the power generated by social classes. As a consequence, the fact of bureaucracy, and state bureaucracy in particular, has always posed a thorny problem for Marxist theory. This problem has become a lot more worrisome since the advent of socialist societies in which an imperious state and party bureaucracy is always very much in evidence. Things would be so much easier for the theory if the political bosses only had the decency to own, and not merely control, the giant press that squeezed the surplus product from the workers. Weber did not survive quite long enough to apply his mind to the analysis of an established socialist society. Had he done so he would have found ample confirmation for his view that without private property and the market, classes could not flourish, but bureaucracy could rise in triumph over all.

III

The third aspect of the distribution of power is party. It would be reasonable to suppose that in including it in the same company as class and status, Weber intended to consider party as a vehicle of power in the distributive set-up. Parties could, in principle, be seen as agencies that are empowered to alter the opportunity structure in various ways. With a change in the political colouring of the party in control, some redistribution of the cake between the classes is always a possibility. But this is not a train of thought that Weber takes up. Far from contemplating the different effects that parties of the right and parties of the left might have upon the stratification order, he betrays a deep scepticism about the ability of any party to make a serious dent in the *status quo*. Once a society had reached the bureaucratic stage there was not much that could be done in the way of radical social engineering. Even revolutionary parties, upon assuming power, would soon be forced to come to terms with the stern and intransigent facts of bureaucratic life. It was therefore wholly characteristic of Weber, to dismiss the

eizure of power by the Bolsheviks as a political non-event. Lenin and
is men would meet with scant success in their attempt to dismantle
he state apparatus and social order bequeathed them by Czarism.[21]
Weber's judgement on the revolution was completely in line with his
usual inclination to downgrade the role of ideas or ideology in political
ction – a far cry from the Weber who is so often advertised as the
aragon of normative sociology.

Parties could not change things very much; nor, it seems, were they
eckoned to be important sources of political ideas and identity. At any
ate, Weber has little if anything to say about the relationship between
he political outlook and aims of a social class and the party it tradi-
ionally supports. He would undoubtedly have been familiar with
Kautsky's well-known thesis about the connection between party and
lass. This argued that the proletarian party was largely responsible for
he development of class consciousness among the workers. The party
was the vehicle that transmitted socialist ideas to the masses, converting
heir inchoate sentiments and gut feelings into an intellectually co-
erent world view. It was the party that really brought about the
ransition from a class in-itself to a class for-itself. Party made all the
ifference in the world.

Weber makes no direct comment on Kautsky's thesis. Since he held
he socialist party and most of its leaders in some disdain, maybe he felt
hat it, and they, would be incapable of bringing enlightenment to
nyone.[22] But in any case this was not the way in which he generally
hought of parties. Far from being progenitors and carriers of class
onsciousness, parties were to some extent the victim of it. He once
xpressed the view that if society became riven by deep ideological
nd class divisions the political atmosphere would be too poisonous for
arties to survive in.

> Two-party systems are impossible in industrialized states, if
> only because of the split in the modern economic strata into
> bourgeoisie and proletariat and because of the meaning of
> socialism as a mass gospel. This creates, as it were, a 'denomi-
> national', barrier . . .[23]

What Weber did not go on to ask is whether the 'denominational
arrier' could possibly have been erected by the parties themselves.
t could easily be argued that political parties thrive and flourish in an
deologically supercharged atmosphere and that they have a vested
nterest in portraying the conflict between themselves and their oppo-
ents as a Manichaen struggle between the forces of light and darkness.
arties, Weber says, "live in a house of 'power'".[24] They also seem to

live quite comfortably in a house of ideology, a house very largely of their own construction.

If parties have very little scope for doing more than tinker with the margins of society; and if they do not serve as the moral instructors and political co-ordinators of social classes, what exactly do they do? More specifically, what do they do that justifies their place in the trinity of power? The short answer is: very little. As far as the reward structure and distributive system is concerned, parties are mainly of interest to Weber for the way in which they dole out perks and privileges within their own ranks. He identifies two different types of party — parties of patronage and parties of principle. Patronage parties are those that have no strong moral commitments and clearly stated aims. They simply tailor their political programme to whatever seems most likely to appeal to the whims of the electorate. Once in office they set about dividing up the spoils among themselves and their key supporters.

Parties of principle, on the other hand, espouse firm doctrine and do not conduct themselves in a purely opportunistic fashion. Weber declares that there is a marked tendency for this type of party to become heavily bureaucratized, for all the reasons elaborated by Michels.[25] Partly as a consequence of this, parties of principle are more than likely to slide down the same slippery path as patronage parties. That is, they become far more intent upon lining the pockets of their own officials and activists than in fulfilling their election pledges and implementing their proclaimed ideals. Even the socialist party, the ideal-typical party of principle, was ultimately self-serving. Despite the party's lofty rhetoric and grand ideals the underlying motives of its followers were "predominantly base."[26] Beneath all the clamour about justice and equality and the dignity of man, what the party zealots were really after was "adventure, victory, booty, power and spoils".[27] Once again, Weber shows how ludicrous he regards the notion that men's actions could be inspired by anything so intangible as values and ideas.

Notwithstanding all their incorrigible cant and self-seeking, Weber did not regard parties as a complete write-off. There was one useful and constructive task they could still perform for the benefit of all: they could set up the political machinery for the selection of outstanding leaders. Weber's comparative analysis of party systems is couched largely in terms of the ability of different systems to foster worthy and responsible leadership. Responsible leaders were those who were willing to elevate national interests above petty class or sectional interests. He believed there were two "fundamentally differing and irreconcilably opposed maxims" of political conduct: one based on the ethic of responsibility' and the other on the 'ethic of ultimate ends'.[28] Political leaders who subscribe to an ethic of responsibility are willing to take account of the "average deficiencies of people".[29] They advocate solutions to problems which have some foreseeable chance of succeeding. They are ready to make certain compromises, to settle for less than they would ideally like, in order to attain their not too ambitious goals. By contrast, those who are committed to an ethic of ultimate ends have an unrealistically heroic view of man. They would rather go down to defeat than accept the ignominy of compromise. By asking too much they lose all. They are, dare one say it?, slightly crazy. Take syndicalists for example:

> You may demonstrate to a convinced syndicalist, believing in an ethic of ultimate ends, that his action will result in increasing the opportunities of reaction, in increasing the oppression of his class, and obstructing its ascent — and you will not make the slightest impression upon him ... The believer in an ethic of ultimate ends feels 'responsible' only for seeing to it that the flame of pure intentions is not quelched: for example, the flame of protesting against the injustices of the social order. To rekindle the flame ever anew is the purpose of his quite irrational deeds, judged in view of their possible success. They are acts that can and shall have only exemplary value.[30]

The thought of Weber berating a militant syndicalist for lack of political acumen is a beguiling one. The syndicalist, for his part, might well have felt that he had heard it all before. There would not be much novelty in being told by a bourgeois, albeit a well-meaning one, that protest against social injustices was likely to be counter-productive as well as hopeless, and was therefore ultimately irrational. It has been the standard conservative refrain from time immemorial. In Weber's case it sprang from a reasoned pessimism about the possibility of radical change in the bureaucratic era. So strong was his conviction that bureaucracy, once set up, could not be dismantled, and that socialist democracy was a pipe dream, he was bound to think that those who taught the opposite were, like his syndicalist friend, sadly lacking in rationality, or, like Rosa Luxemburg, specimens that belonged in the "zoological gardens".[31] People like her, especially committed as he was to an ethic of ultimate ends, would lead the working class to disaster by setting it impossible political tasks. Far better the cautious and moderating touch of the trade union leaders or the Bernstein revisionists, honourable men who were well-practised in the arts of responsibility'.

Weber's distaste for Rosa Luxemburg's brand of politics extende
to matters of party organization. She was a strong advocate of mas
rank and file participation in party affairs. The duty of the part
leadership was to organize and channel the political spontaneity of th
masses; workers had to be directly involved in all important decision
lest the leadership become remote and puffed-up. Weber was of precisel
the opposite view. Rather like Lenin, he believed that party polic
and the machinery of decision-making should be kept in the hands c
a virtuoso elite. "Political action" he wrote, "is always determined b
the 'principle of small numbers', that means, the superior politica
manoeuverability of small leading groups. In-mass states, this caesaris
element is ineradicable."[32] Since party politics was properly th
business of elites rather than masses it followed that members an
supporters should be content to play a passive and docile role. Webe
had no time for fancy proposals designed to encourage inner-part
democracy by making the leadership more accountable to the ran
and file. It was the duty of leaders to lay down the party line and fo
others to obey. Weber had quite a Teutonic streak in him.

What he also had in him were firm ideas about the sort of me
who were best fitted for party leadership. They were the men wh
lived 'for' politics and not 'off' politics. Those who lived off politic
were either the grey salaried officials or the unprincipled booty hunters
They were not the stuff of which great leaders were made; they wer
too liable to kow-tow to the party machine or to court cheap popu
larity. Genuine leaders could only emerge from among those few wh
lived 'for' politics, in particular men of independent means who coul
afford to back their own convictions and risk the displeasure of th
party hacks.

The all-important question for Weber was: "Do the parties in
fully developed mass democracy permit at all the rise of men wit
leadership capacities?"[33] His great fear was that the tawdry concer
with 'vote-grabbing' and the terrible grip of the party apparatus, woul
put paid to the chances of men of independent judgement and rar
quality; men, perhaps, not altogether unlike himself? He certainly fel
he had a constructive role to play in German politics in the post-wa
era. When in fact his chance did finally come he was humiliatingl
outmanoevred by the party bosses. This rejection put paid to hi
lingering political ambitions. It could not have done much either t
allay his worst fears on the leadership question.

Suggestions for Further Reading

For the reader tackling Weber for the first time, it might be best to start with *The Protestant Ethic and the Spirit of Capitalism* (Allen and Unwin). This essay nicely captures Weber's characteristic blend of learning, insight and ambiguity. Any serious acquaintance with his work must involve coming to grips with *Economy and Society* (Bedminster Press) but it would be as well to delay this until some of its leading themes have been explored elsewhere. An invaluable guide here is Reinhard Bendix, *Max Weber: An Intellectual Portrait* (Doubleday). Equally good is the selection of extracts in H. H. Gerth and C. Wright Mills, *From Max Weber* (Routledge). After this preparation there should be no difficulty with Weber's other main works, the most important among them being: *The Methodology of the Social Sciences* (Free Press); *The Religion of India, The Religion of China,* and *Ancient Judaism* (all Free Press); and the *General Economic History* (FreePress/Collier).

There is a mountain of literature on or about Weber. The source of most commentaries on his life and career is Marianne Weber, *Max Weber: A Biography* (Wiley). Sadly, this cannot be recommended as an absorbing read; it is too heavily weighted down by large chunks of lacklustre family correspondence. A much better bet is Donald MacRae,

Weber (Fontana) or Arthur Mitzman, *The Iron Cage* (Knopf). Mitzman's book is a kind of psycho-biography that puts forward beguiling and only mildly outrageous views about the link between Weber's theories and his inner turmoil.

The outstanding work on Weber's political ideas is David Beetham, *Max Weber and the Theory of Modern Politics* (Allen and Unwin). Also good in this field are: Ilse Dronberger, *The Political Thought of Max Weber* (Appleton Century Croft), W. J. Mommsen, *The Age of Bureaucracy* (Blackwell) and Anthony Giddens, *Politics and Sociology in the Thought of Max Weber* (Macmillan).

In the field of religion, two recent books deserve special mention: Bryan S. Turner, *Weber and Islam* (Routledge) and Gordon Marshall, *Presbyteries and Profits* (Clarendon Press). Marshall's book presents one of the best cases likely to be made in defence of the Protestant ethic thesis.

Among the many general commentaries and interpretations of Weber's work, the following are especially worth noting: Talcott Parsons, *The Structure of Social Action* (Free Press). This is the *locus classicus* of the view of Weber as the leading exemplar of normative sociology. A valuable counterweight to Parsons' approach is Anthony Giddens, *Capitalism and Modern Social Theory* (Cambridge). Also useful are Reinhard Bendix and Guenther Roth, *Scholarship and Partisanship* (California); W. G. Runciman, *A Critique of Max Weber's Philosophy of Social Science* (Cambridge); Julien Freund, *The Sociology of Max Weber* (Allen Lane); Dennis H. Wrong (Ed.) *Max Weber* (Prentice Hall); and Otto Stammer (Ed.) *Max Weber and Sociology Today* (Blackwell). This last book is a collection of essays arising from a conference held in Heidelberg in 1964 to commemorate the centenary of Weber's birth. Judging by the undertone of political accusation directed at Weber by some of the contributors, Nuremburg might have been a more appropriate venue.

Notes

Chapter 1

[1]   Max Weber, *Economy and Society* (Eds. Guenther Roth and Claus Wittich) Bedminster Press, New York (1968), p. 13.

[2]   *ibid*, p. 13.

[3]   *ibid*, p. 14.

[4]   See, for example, Alfred Schutz (Collected Papers I). *The Problem of Social Reality*, Martinus Nijhoff, The Hague, (1967), pp. 62–63.

[5]   Weber, *Economy and Society*, p. 5.

[6]   Weber, *ibid*, p. 9.

[7]   *ibid*, p. 8.

[8]   *ibid*, p. 9.

[9]   *ibid*, pp. 10–11.

[10] *ibid*, p. 12.

[11] Positivists might reasonably respond that they do not require instruction in this matter since they do not normally try to correlate things like increases in the birth rate with increases in the stork population.

[12] Weber, *ibid*, p. 8.

[13]   *ibid*, pp. 5-6. Weber goes on to hint that we might be able to grasp things 'intellectually' that we cannot understand 'empathically'. This enigmatic remark is not pursued, which is just as well perhaps.

[14]   *ibid*, p. 6.

[15]   Peter Winch, *The Idea of a Social Science*, Routledge, London, 1958, p. 88. Durkheim dismissed this sort of argument as a "mystical doctrine". It could satisfy only those "who prefer to think with their feelings and emotions rather than with their understanding." Emile Durkheim, *The Rules of Sociological Method*, Free Press, Glencoe, (1938), pp. 33-34.

[16]   Max Weber, *The Protestant Ethic and the Spirit of Capitalism*, Allen and Unwin, London, (1930), p. 233.

[17]   Weber, *Economy and Society*, p. 16.

[18]   Weber, *ibid*, p. 6.

[19]   Although religious zeal and political fanaticism are thought to be beyond the reach of the unsympathetic observer's understanding, the same does not seem to hold for emotional intensity in general. "The more we ourselves are susceptible to such emotional reactions as anxiety, anger, ambition, envy ... and appetites of all sorts ... the more readily we can empathize with them. Even when such emotions are found in a degree of intensity of which the observer himself is completely incapable, he can still have a significant degree of emotional understanding of their meaning and can interpret intellectually their influence on the course of action ..."
       ibid, p. 6.

[20]   *ibid*, pp. 21-22.

[21]   Karl Marx, *Capital* Vol. III, Foreign Languages Publishing Moscow, (1959), p. 797.

[22]   Emile Durkheim, *Suicide*, Routledge, London, (1952), p. 170.

[23]   Max Weber, *The Methodology of the Social Sciences*, Free Press, New York, (1949), p. 43.

[24]   Weber, *ibid*, p. 90.

[25]   *ibid*, p. 81.

[26]   *ibid*, p. 72.

[27]   Emile Durkheim, *The Rules of Sociological Method*, p. 31. Naturally Durkheim never followed this bad piece of advice. It would be difficult to think of a sociologist whose work is more thoroughly infused with definite preconceptions than his.

[28]   Weber could not quite make up his mind on this crucial point. Generally he seems willing to accept that it is possible to con-

struct more than one ideal-type of any given phenomenon. Occasionally, though, he suggests that the explanatory value of an ideal-type depended upon its being a 'correct' formulation. See for example, *The Methodology of the Social Sciences*, p. 102.

[29] *ibid*, p. 97.
[30] *ibid*, p. 57.
[31] *ibid*, p. 11.
[32] *ibid*, p. 58.
[33] A good example of the *genre* in the analysis of news and current affairs on television is the work of the the Glasgow University Media Group, *Bad News* and *More Bad News*, Routledge, London, (1976 and 1980).
[34] Weber, *Economy and Society*, p. 973.
[35] *ibid*, p. 975.
[36] Among the classic accounts are, Robert K. Merton, "Bureaucratic Structure and Personality", in his *Social Theory and Social Structure*, Free Press, Glencoe, (1957); Philip Selznick, *TVA and the Grass Roots*, University of California Press, Berkeley, (1953); Peter M. Blau, *Bureaucracy in Modern Society*, Random House, New York, (1956); Alvin W. Gouldner, *Patterns of Industrial Bureaucracy*, Free Press, Glencoe, (1954).
[37] Weber, *Economy and Society*, p. 6.
[38] Weber, *The Methodology of the Social Sciences*, pp. 184-5. These terms have their origin in an abstruse and deservedly forgotten debate among German historians.
[39] Leon Trotsky, *Diary in Exile*, Harvard University Press, (1976), p. 46.

Chapter 2

[1] Max Weber, *The Protestant Ethic and the Spirit of Capitalism*, Allen and Unwin, London, (1930), pp. 17-22.
[2] *ibid*, p. 40.
[3] *ibid*, p. 180.
[4] *ibid*, p. 91.
[5] *ibid*, p. 91.
[6] *ibid*, p. 114.
[7] *ibid*, p. 115.
[8] Max Weber, *General Economic History*, Collier Books New York, (1961), p. 267.

[9] *The Protestant Ethic*, p. 192. Elsewhere he writes "The external courses of religious behaviour are so diverse that an understanding of this behaviour can only be achieved from the viewpoint of the subjective experiences, ideas, and purposes of the individuals concerned — in short from the viewpoint of the religious behaviour's 'meaning'". *Economy and Society*. p. 399.

[10] *ibid*, p. 259.

[11] *ibid*, pp. 109–110.

[12] *ibid*, p. 110.

[13] *ibid*, p. 111.

[14] *ibid*, p. 116.

[15] *ibid*, pp. 116–117.

[16] *ibid*, p. 85.

[17] *ibid*, p. 82.

[18] "Antikritisches Schlusswort zum 'Geist des Kapitalismus'" *Archiv für Sozialwissenschaft und Sozialpolitik*, **31**, No. 2, (1910), p. 593.

[19] *The Protestant Ethic*, p. 162.

[20] *ibid*, p. 162.

[21] *ibid*, p. 60.

[22] *ibid*, p. 62.

[23] *ibid*, p. 62.

[24] *ibid*, p. 177.

[25] In his *Antikritisches Schlusswort*, Weber refers to the Calvinist artisan or worker "whose diligence and conscientiousness in his God-ordained calling revealed his state of grace." *op. cit.*, p. 593.

[26] *Economy and Society*, p. 468 and p. 470.

[27] *ibid*, p. 472.

[28] *ibid*, p. 479.

[29] *ibid*, p. 483.

[30] *ibid*, p. 476.

[31] *ibid*, pp. 483–484.

[32] *The Protestant Ethic*, p. 281.

[33] *Economy and Society*, p. 1010.

[34] John Kenneth Galbraith, *The Nature of Mass Poverty*, Harvard University Press, (1979).

[35] *The Protestant Ethic*, p. 131.

[36] *ibid*, pp. 156–157.

[37] *ibid*, p. 157.

[38] *ibid*, p. 172.

[39]   *ibid*, p. 183.
[40]   *From Max Weber* (eds. H. H. Gerth and C. Wright Mills) Rout-
       ledge, London, (1948), pp. 308–309.
[41]   *Economy and Society*, p. 491.
[42]   *ibid*, p. 477.
[43]   *From Max Weber*, pp. 304–305.
[44]   *ibid*, p. 305.
[45]   *ibid*, p. 319.
[46]   In his reply to his critics, Weber repeats the story of the Baptist
       banker and again makes the point that this aspect of sect be-
       haviour was a survival of earlier and commoner practices. "Anti-
       kritisches Schlusswort", *op cit.*, pp. 585–586.
[47]   *From Max Weber*, p. 321.
[48]   *The Religion of India*, Free Press, New York, (1958), p. 112.
[49]   Milton Singer, *When a Great Tradition Modernizes*, Pall Mall
       Press, London (1972).
[50]   Maxime Rodinson, *Islam and Capitalism*, Allen Lane, London,
       1974; Bryan S. Turner, *Weber and Islam*, Routledge, London,
       (1974).
[51]   Werner Sombart, *The Quintessence of Capitalism*, New York,
       (1967); *The Jews and Modern Capitalism*, Free Press, Glencoe,
       (1951).
[52]   *The Religion of India*, pp. 3–4.
[53]   *The Religion of China*, Free Press, New York, (1951), p. 248.
[54]   *ibid*, p. 249.
[55]   Talcott Parsons, "Introduction" to Max Weber, *The Sociology
       of Religion*, Methuen, London, (1965), pp. xxi–xxii.
[56]   *Economy and Society*, pp. 1212–1262.
[57]   *ibid*, p. 1237.
[58]   *ibid*, p. 847.
[59]   *The Protestant Ethic*, pp. 14–16.
[60]   Gordon Marshall, *Presbyteries and Profits: Calvinism and the
       Development of Capitalism in Scotland, 1560–1707*, Clarendon
       Press, Oxford, (1980).
[61]   *ibid*, pp. 273–275.
[62]   *ibid*, p. 276.

Chapter 3

[1]   Max Weber, *Economy and Society*, p. 941.
[2]   *ibid*, p. 904.
[3]   *ibid*, p. 911.

[4]   Max Weber, "Politics as a Vocation", in H. H. Gerth and C.
      Wright Mills, *From Max Weber*, Routledge, London, (1948),
      pp. 77-78.
[5]   *Economy and Society*, pp. 943-6.
[6]   *ibid.* p. 946.
[7]   *ibid*, p. 946.
[8]   *ibid*, p. 946.
[9]   *ibid*, p. 954.
[10] *ibid*, p. 214.
[11] *ibid*, p. 214.
[12] "Politics as a Vocation", p. 78.
[13] *Economy and Society*, p. 953.
[14] "Politics as a Vocation", p. 78.
[15] *Economy and Society*, p. 946.
[16] Etzioni's typology of command and compliance is the out-
      standing work in this field. A. Etzioni, *A Comparative Analysis
      of Complex Organizations*. Free Press, New York, (1961).
[17] *Economy and Society*, pp. 946-7.
[18] *ibid*, p. 1012.
[19] *ibid*, p. 1028.
[20] *ibid*, p. 1041.
[21] *ibid*, p. 1072.
[22] *ibid*, p. 1082.
[23] *ibid*, pp. 1407-1408 (italics added).
[24] *ibid.*, p. 1111.
[25] *ibid*, p. 1133.
[26] *ibid*, p. 1117.
[27] *ibid*, p. 1116.
[28] *ibid*, p. 1132.
[29] *ibid*, p. 1132.
[30] Peter M. Blau, "Critical Remarks on Weber's Theory of Author-
      ity", in Dennis H. Wrong, (Ed.) *Max Weber*, Prentice Hall,
      Englewood Cliffs, New Jersey, (1970), p. 153.
[31] *Economy and Society*, p. 1133.
[32] *ibid*, p. 1393.
[33] *ibid*, p. 1417.
[34] *ibid*, pp. 1418.

Chapter 4

[1]   Max Weber, *Economy and Society*, p. 927.
[2]   *ibid*, p. 927.
[3]   *ibid*, pp. 729–30.
[4]   *ibid*, p. 928.
[5]   Weber argued that there would be less freedom for workers under social ownership than under private capitalism, "since every power struggle with a state bureaucracy is hopeless and since there is no appeal to an agency which as a matter of principle would be interested in limiting the employer's power, such as there is in the case of private enterprise ... State bureaucracy would rule *alone* if private capitalism were eliminated. The private and public bureaucracies which now work next to, and potentially against, each other and hence check one another to a degree, would be merged into a single hierarchy. This would be similar to the situation in ancient Egypt, but it would occur in a much more rational – and hence unbreakable – form." *ibid*, p. 1402.
[6]   Karl Marx, *The Poverty of Philosophy*, Martin Lawrence, London, (1936), p. 92.
[7]   *Economy and Society*, p. 1091.
[8]   Heribert Adam has pointed out that the capitalist mode of production in South Africa has adapted to the system of *apartheid* instead of dismantling it. On a Marxist analysis, "the artificially chained forces of production are not allowed their full development within an outdated institutional frame of race laws and, therefore, must inevitably burst apart these modes of production." *Modernizing Racial Domination*, University of California Press, Berkeley (1971), p. 146. Herbert Blumer also argued that industrial capitalism is more likely to accommodate itself to a racially stratified system than to re-order it. "Industrialization and Race Relations", in Guy Hunter (Ed.) *Industrialization and Race Relations*, Oxford University Press, London, (1965).
[9]   *Economy and Society*, p. 936.
[10] See, for example, Kenneth Prandy, *Professional Employees*, Faber, London, (1965).
[11] *Economy and Society*, p. 935.
[12] For a recent re-statement of this position, see Daniel Bell, "Ethnicity and Social Change", in Nathan Glazer and Daniel P. Moynihan (Eds.) *Ethnicity*, Harvard University Press, (1975).
[13] *Economy and Society*, p. 391.

118   Max Weber

[14]   *ibid*, p. 938.
[15]   There is a fuller discussion of Weber's concept of social closure in my *Marxism and Class Theory: A Bourgeois Critique*, Tavistock, London, (1979).
[16]   *Economy and Society*, p. 342.
[17]   *ibid*, p. 1000.
[18]   *ibid*, p. 342.
[19]   *ibid*, pp. 988–89.
[20]   An excellent account of Weber's views on all this, and much else besides, is to be found in David Beetham, *Max Weber and the Theory of Modern Politics*, Allen and Unwin, London, (1974), Chapter 6.
[21]   Weber thought that the life of the new Soviet state "was to be reckoned in months" rather than years. This was partly to do with the fact that the Bolshevik regime was a "military dictatorship ... not of generals but of *corporals*". Weber obviously could not believe in the survival of a society that was controlled by the lower ranks. The revolution was inspired not by notions of justice and freedom but by the lust for booty. Max Weber, *Gesammelte Politische Schriften*, (Ed. Johannes Winckelmann) J. C. B. Mohr, Tübingen, (1971), pp. 292–3.
[22]   Weber does state, in a brief note, that workers are more likely to attain class consciousness "if they are led toward readily understood goals, which are imposed and interpreted by men outside their class (intelligentsia)." There is, however, no specific mention of the role of the party. *Economy and Society*, p. 305.
[23]   *ibid*, p. 1443.
[24]   Roth and Wittich translate this as "sphere" of power, *Economy and Society*, p. 938; Gerth and Mills render it as "house" of power, *From Max Weber*, p. 194. The original text reads as follows: "Während die 'Klassen' in der 'Wirtschaftsordnung', die 'Stände' in der sozialen Ordnung ... ihre eigentliche Heimat haben ... sind 'Parteien' in der Sphäre der 'Macht' zu Hause." Max Weber *Wirtschaft und Gesellschaft* (Ed. Johannes Winckelmann) J. C. B. Mohr, Tübingen, (1976), p. 539.
[25]   Robert Michels, *Political Parties*, Free Press, Glencoe, (1958).
[26]   "Politics as a Vocation" in *From Max Weber*, p. 125.
[27]   *ibid*, p. 125.
[28]   *ibid*, p. 120.
[29]   *ibid*, p. 121.
[30]   *ibid*, pp. 120–21.

[31] In a speech in Karslruhe in January 1919, shortly before Luxem-
      burg was done away with by the forces of law and order. Cited
      in Wolfgang J. Mommsen, *Max Weber und die deutsche Politik,
      1890–1920*, J. C. B. Mohr, Tübingen, (1959), p. 300.
[32] *Economy and Society*, p. 1414.
[33] *ibid*, p. 1458.

Index